THE
BALANCED
LIFE METHOD

THE 7-PILLAR BLUEPRINT
TO LASTING HEALTH
AND WELLNESS

LORI NOLAN

WHAT PEOPLE ARE SAYING ABOUT THE **BALANCED** LIFE METHOD

The technological advances in the practice of modern medicine are concerned only with healing the physical body. While integral in the healing of disease, physical healing satisfies only one aspect of wellness. These advances do not exempt the patient from the responsibility of defining their own wellness and ensuring that each day, they take one more step towards their own goals. In *The Balanced Life Method,* Nolan offers a beautiful story of vulnerability, faith, and trust, as well as a practical road map to walk the path of wholeness, in which the needs of the physical, mental, emotional, and spiritual body find solace.

—Dr. Rachel Brooks Fashano

Lori Nolan clearly understands that a balanced and healthy life begins within yourself first. This book will lay an essential spiritual foundation that will catapult you into the mental and physical wholeness we all want. On every page, you will hear her voice of wisdom and encouragement as she leads you to build your whole self into overall wellness and newfound joy!

—Joan Dunnam
Author of *As Christ Loves the Church* and
A 5-Week Study To An Extraordinary Marriage

If you are looking for a practical, God-led process to bring your life into balance, Lori Nolan can help equip you for the journey. Lori's 7 pillars were the stepping stones to wellness that I needed to take control of my health and chart a new course. I overate, obsessed about food, mistreated my body and mind, and—worst of all—had no hope that I could ever change. But that wasn't true. Little by little I began to embrace my health and my outlook to chart the course toward a better future. Is my life perfect now? No, but with God's grace and Lori's help, I made a 180-degree turn, and I haven't looked back. I am still on the journey to health and wellness but am now equipped for the journey. I have Lori Nolan to thank for that. I am confident she can help you, too.

—Rhonda Brooks
Former editorial director, *Farm Journal Media*

Lori Nolan's insightful book offers a holistic approach to wellness with practical advice and profound biblical wisdom. Her work uplifts the soul, guiding readers toward a harmonious and fulfilling life. This book is a must-read for everyone!

—Stacy Jo Coffee-Thorne
Author
CEO of *Freedom Support Solutions*
President of *Association of Christian Business Women*

In a world teeming with fleeting health trends and superficial wellness fads, *The Balanced Life Method* emerges as a fresh voice full of wisdom, blending physical well-being with the essential aspects of spiritual nourishment. This book is not merely a guide; it's a journey into the heart of holistic health, where the convergence of body, soul, and spirit becomes the foundation for a full and abundant life. Through personal stories, grounded insights, and a deep understanding of the human spirit, Lori masterfully illustrates how our wellness is not just about what we consume or how well we exercise but about nurturing a fully devoted relationship with our inner selves and our Creator.

It reminds us of the powerful Scripture in 3 John 1:2, "Dear friend, I pray that you may enjoy good health and that all may go well with you, even as your soul is getting along well." This verse captures the theme of *The Balanced Life Method*, a call to care for our entire selves in a manner that honors God with our bodies and fosters our physical vitality.

Whether you're seeking to heal from within, aiming to align your life with your core values, or simply aspiring to a well-paced and balanced life, *The Balanced Life Method* will give you the wisdom, tools, and spiritual insight to guide you on this noble path. It's more than a book; it's a companion for anyone dedicated to journaling with Christ toward spiritual and physical health.

—Dave Simiele
Campus Pastor, Christ Fellowship Church

In *The Balanced Life Method,* you will experience Lori's passion and wisdom for orchestrating true balance in critical areas of your life. Wherever you are in your life's journey, Lori's 7 pillars will be your guide to navigating your wellness, based on a spiritual foundation.

Lori provides specific direction and helpful advice in overcoming the obstacles that are in your way for improved wellness. This is a must-read for anyone interested in living a fulfilled and optimistic life of wellness.

—Bob Fashano
Author, Executive Coach, International Speaker

Copyright © 2024 by Lori Nolan

Published by Four Rivers Media

All rights reserved. No portion of this book may be reproduced, stored in a retrieval system, or transmitted in any form or by any means—electronic, mechanical, photocopy, recording, scanning, or other—except for brief quotations in critical reviews or articles, without prior written permission of the author.

Unless otherwise specified, all Scripture quotations are from The ESV® Bible (The Holy Bible, English Standard Version®), copyright © 2001 by Crossway, a publishing ministry of Good News Publishers. Used by permission. All rights reserved. | Scripture quotations marked AMP are taken from the Amplified® Bible (AMP), Copyright © 2015 by The Lockman Foundation. Used by permission. www.lockman.org | Scripture quotations marked KJV are taken from the King James Version of the Bible. Public domain. | Scripture quotations marked NIV are taken from the Holy Bible, New International Version®, NIV®. Copyright © 1973, 1978, 1984, 2011 by Biblica, Inc.™ Used by permission of Zondervan. All rights reserved worldwide. www.zondervan.com. The "NIV" and "New International Version" are trademarks registered in the United States Patent and Trademark Office by Biblica, Inc.™ | Scripture quotations marked NKJV are taken from the New King James Version®. Copyright © 1982 by Thomas Nelson. Used by permission. All rights reserved. | Scripture quotations marked NLT are taken from the Holy Bible, New Living Translation, copyright © 1996, 2004, 2015 by Tyndale House Foundation. Used by permission of Tyndale House Publishers, Inc., Carol Stream, Illinois 60188. All rights reserved.

For foreign and subsidiary rights, contact the author.

Cover design by: Sara Young
Cover photo by: Mariah Camacho

ISBN: 978-1-960678-59-1   1 2 3 4 5 6 7 8 9 10

Printed in the United States of America

This book is dedicated to my Lord and Savior, Jesus Christ, apart from whom, I could do nothing. He redeemed my life and put a new purpose in my heart.

To my parents, who have never given up on me but always encouraged, supported, and cheered me on through every season and circumstance of life. Thank you for giving me a firm foundation on which to grow up.

To my husband, children, and grandchildren, who have given me love like I've never known. Your lives have changed me for the better, and I'm beyond grateful to have you all.

To my beautiful friend Sabrina, who introduced me to the world of health coaching. She was promoted to heaven, but I know she would be happy and proud to know her love of helping others lives on in the work I do.

CONTENTS

Preface xi

Acknowledgments xiii

Introduction 15

PILLAR 1 **SPIRIT** 21

PILLAR 2 **NUTRITION** 41

PILLAR 3 **STRESS** 63

PILLAR 4 **SLEEP** 81

PILLAR 5 **FITNESS** 95

PILLAR 6 **RELATIONSHIPS** 111

PILLAR 7 **PURPOSE** 133

Afterword 145

PREFACE

I have been blessed to have a grandmother and a mother who taught me about food, nutrition, and wellness. My grandma had a garden and read *Prevention* magazine back in the day. Kids really do watch because I absorbed all that and just knew to take a papaya enzyme when my stomach was upset—go figure! The love for wellness started way back then for me. As the years went on, I have been fortunate to work in the fitness industry, the business world, and then in the medical field, where I've been able to integrate nutrition into people's wellness plans to help heal them.

Along the way, I learned so many things, but the one that stood out the most was that being healthy and well takes examining and changing many aspects of our lives. Years ago, as a young personal trainer, I couldn't figure out why the middle-aged folks who were faithful to their fitness routines weren't seeing the results they wanted. I guess you could say that was the catalyst that sent me back to school to learn about nutrition and how food works to heal us.

> **WHEN WE EXAMINE THE SEVEN BASIC AREAS THAT HAVE AN IMPACT ON HEALTH, WE CAN FINALLY UNCOVER WHAT'S BEEN OVERLOOKED IN THE PAST, THEN MOVE FORWARD TO FINALLY GET THAT CONTROL AND THE ANSWERS WE HAVE SEARCHED FOR.**

But even then, after working with so many patients in the functional medicine space, I realized there was still more. We needed to address how they were sleeping, the stress they were experiencing, and the factor with the biggest impact across the board—addressing their spirit. We don't really think of that when we are thinking about health. We tend to focus on just the body. But we are a spirit with a body, not the other way around. My passion has become helping people discover the power they have to enjoy the optimal health and wellness that God wants for all of us. When we examine the seven basic areas that have an impact on health, we can finally uncover what's been overlooked in the past, then move forward to finally get that control and the answers we have searched for.

ACKNOWLEDGMENTS

I want to thank my father for his wisdom, support, and encouragement to write this book and be all that I can be so that I may give to others.

Julie Green of Julie Green Ministries International, whose daily teachings on God's Word have brought me to another level of wisdom and revelation.

Amanda Grace of Ark of Grace Ministries, whose prophetic word of hope and teaching has made me grow. Also, for sending me *The Believer's Authority,* a book by Kenneth E. Hagin, which has changed my life forever.

My dear friends and mentors, Ruth and Victor, who God sent into my life at just the perfect time. Your prayers, support, and wisdom have gotten me through some challenging times and helped me to grow.

My home church, Christ Fellowship, and all our pastors on staff that preach and teach. I am so thankful to be part of a church family that stands firm and teaches God's Word unapologetically.

My author coach, Megan, without you, this book could not have been written. Thank you for your guidance and help with taking the message God gave me and translating it into the written word.

All my clients over the years, who have given me the privilege of joining them on their wellness journey and have entrusted me with their personal struggles and intimate parts of their lives. I have learned so much from all of you and am deeply grateful to you.

"Wisdom has built her house; she has set up its seven pillars."
—Proverbs 9:1 (NIV)

INTRODUCTION

As I was writing the last chapter of this book, God opened up the Word to me and led me straight to Proverbs 9:1, the primary verse on which this book is based. Never had I made the connection at the genesis of this book between the 7-Pillared Balanced Life Method and this scripture. Approaching the conclusion of this book, it was this revelation that reinforced what I knew to already be true—the message within the pages of this book is God-breathed, one that I can take no credit for.

> **COINCIDENCE IS NOT IN GOD'S VOCABULARY, AND THAT, MY FRIENDS, IS NO COINCIDENCE.**

Coincidence is not in God's vocabulary, and that, my friends, is no coincidence. And, like my discovery of this scripture, God insists on being intentional in our lives. He cares about you far too much to lead you through this life haphazardly, as if each and every victory you accrue is dumb luck. That you picked up this book is a purposeful move of God's guiding hand. He knows who you are, why you are here, and what you need.

God uses the analogy of a well-built house in the Bible to depict the condition of our lives as either unshakeable or destructible. Luke 6:47–48 (NKJV) says:

"Whoever comes to Me, and hears My sayings and does them, I will show you whom he is like: He is like a man building a house, who dug deep and laid the foundation on the rock. And when the flood arose, the stream beat vehemently against that house, and could not shake it, for it was founded on the rock."

Jesus refers to Himself as "the Rock" and how a house (symbolic of your life) cannot stand without Him. This teaching tells us something very important about the balanced life: it's a house that will either collapse or stand firm against the elements, all hinging on what we are building our house on. It is the difference between fleeting success and long-lasting change. Without a strong foundation, the entire structure is compromised, and that house will only stand for so long. So it is with wellness. My intention is to equip you with everything you need to build that house—one that cannot and will not be shaken.

So, who are you, reader?

Well, I imagine that you're someone like me, wanting to be healthy, happy, and full of energy to live life. I like to be in control of my health, and I'm sure you do as well. There is nothing worse than waking up one day and realizing you don't feel like you used to feel. If you've picked up this book with the hopes of learning something—new truths, such as your body was designed to work holistically (it's all connected!)—I promise you that you will. Achieving overall wellness requires looking at the whole picture. We get blasted with "the new fad nutrition of the day," "the new fad workout of the day," or "take this and try that," which leaves the majority of us asking questions and leaving frustrated. I'm going to uncover some truths that you can take away that I know will spark some hope. The kind of hope that leaves you knowing you are in control.

The majority of us are on social media, and we get inundated with countless suggestions of how to achieve happiness and health. There are plenty of experts who offer suggestions that, quite frankly, are overwhelming. When we get overwhelmed, most of us tend to freeze and continue doing what we are doing out of confusion. While the advice and tips may be great, they may not be right for us, and sometimes, tuning all that out may be the biggest help. We could lose hope and even trust in someone we thought would give us good advice. The cycle just continues, and the old way of coping never gets unlearned. As a result, we quit as soon as we realize that the prescription didn't work.

I have been right where you are, searching, hoping, and praying, and sometimes, feeling even downright discouraged, wondering if I could possibly get hold of my health and my life and find balance. As a woman, I have been through many stages of life: the childbearing years, raising children, working, being a single mom, and now onto my next chapter. Men also go through similar phases of life, which leave them struggling and searching for that balance.

It was on my own journey in life that I started putting the seven pillars into practice: spirituality, nutrition, stress, sleep, fitness, relationships, and purpose. I had to do some self-examination regarding past trauma and choices I had made and be transparent with myself and God (even though He already knew and was waiting on me). I had to inspect some deep things in my life, like unforgiveness and parts of me that needed some inner spiritual healing so that the physical things I was dealing with could heal and improve. It was then that I realized how synergistically these areas all work together, and I couldn't focus on just one and not the other. Or, I thought I had one nailed down, only to discover I had to readjust (like my fitness routine and the foods I was eating). God always wants to give us more revelation and wisdom.

> **GOD ALWAYS WANTS TO GIVE US MORE REVELATION AND WISDOM.**

When we position ourselves to partner with Him, He will do just that. Whether you're a man or woman, you will go through these seasons like I have. You will have to navigate all the changes your body is making—not just hormonal (men and women both experience a "pause")—but your emotional capacity to manage life events and even your spiritual growth. I will be sharing many of my own and my clients' personal stories with the hopes that you will be able to identify with them. Like you, I, too, want success in the important areas of life, such as healthy relationships, managing stress, living my purpose, and having a deeper relationship with my Creator, and so do the clients I work with personally and in groups.

Besides all the social media influencers out there, there are loads of books, resources, and magazines that have a lot to say about the topic of successfully finding a healthy and balanced life, but keep this one important fact in mind: only you know you the best. I believe we all know the answer to achieving overall health and wellness in our own lives but may need some basic guidance to find that answer, and that's what this book is designed to do—not promote a diet or fitness routine or offer that quick fix—but design a simple solution to making changes that will last a lifetime using the seven primary pillars of health.

The 7-pillar approach gives you a simple blueprint to follow for each area of your life, just like it gave me. These seven areas are common to most adults and basic drivers of overall wellness. For example, you can eat a perfect organic diet and work out six days a week but still feel completely awful and can't figure out why. What if something needs tweaking, or what if you discover that it's really some unaddressed and underlying chronic stress or past trauma creating and enabling the imbalance?

I reference the Bible often because our health is important to God but also because He is the Author of life with the best answers for us. We are most useful in fulfilling His purposes for our lives when we are experiencing His *shalom* (wholeness, soundness, peace, and health). Having a balanced life is like building a house. First, you need a solid foundation to build on (spirit). Next, you frame the structure (nutrition, stress, sleep, and fitness). Finally, you install your roof (relationships and purpose). If a house is built properly, it will be a solid, balanced structure that will last.

After working with many people over the years (both in the fitness world and the medical field), I've had the privilege of seeing people make amazing transformations in their health and relationships and start living their lives with purpose and passion. Just examining your nutrition or fitness isn't enough. It is only when you examine and balance these seven areas that you will discover how to achieve overall wellness that *lasts*. It's amazing to uncover spiritual issues such as unforgiveness or even bitterness that contribute to mental health issues and disrupt your relationships or to stumble upon hidden guilt, shame, or self-worth that contribute to being overweight.

> **OUR GENES DON'T DICTATE OUR DESTINY, AND, SURPRISINGLY, A LOT OF PEOPLE DON'T KNOW THAT.**

When we finally discover the truth—that we have the power and authority to control every outcome of our lives—it's the best revelation ever! When people feel empowered, there's no stopping them. We all want to live a healthy life that we feel in control of. Our genes don't dictate our destiny, and, surprisingly, a lot of people don't know that.

Get ready to learn some very simple steps to discover just how much power you have to transform your health and start living life the way God intended.

> *"Beloved, I pray that all may go well with you and that you may be in good health, as it goes well with your soul."*
> —3 John 1:2

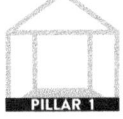

PILLAR 1

SPIRIT

He just couldn't keep the weight off, his cholesterol down, and his stress under control, let alone the sleep hygiene we discussed during our sessions. It was a never-ending cycle of climbing the mountain, getting to the top, then falling back down again. Everything would appear on point, but he never seemed able to achieve true success. So, what was going on with this guy?

This client was someone I'll say I attempted to work with, who thought he was ready to jump in but just never got the results he wanted. You may be wondering what our spirit and spirituality have to do with a balanced life, health, and wellness? Excellent question! The case I just mentioned has everything to do with it, and we'll soon see why. When I ask people what they think of when they hear the word "spirit," the first thing that comes to *most* people's minds (because I ask them) is some afterlife entity, like a ghost, or an upbeat mood like when you're watching your favorite sports team play. But when you look up the word spirit, the first thing that comes up is the noun definition: "the principle of conscious life, the vital principle in humans, animating the body or mediating between body and soul."[1] So, in other words,

---

1 "Spirit Definition & Usage Examples," *Dictionary.Com*, www.dictionary.com/browse/spirit, accessed 29 Mar. 2024.

it is our spirit that makes everything happen in the body and soul (mind, will, and emotions).

> **I BELIEVE A LOT OF PEOPLE HAVE THE MISCONCEPTION THAT WE ARE A BODY THAT HAS A SPIRIT AND SOUL, BUT THE REALITY IS, WE ARE A SPIRIT THAT HAS A BODY AND SOUL.**

I want to get this straight at the beginning of this book because I believe a lot of people have the misconception that we are a body that *has* a spirit and soul, but the reality is, we *are* a spirit that has a body and soul. This is a key concept to embrace throughout this book. Our body and our soul are directly affected by our spirit. We live in a world that is hyperfocused on looking good and feeling good, and we chase our wellness. As I mentioned in the introduction, I have been in both the fitness and medical fields, and I'm telling you, the emphasis has always been on looking good and feeling good. While both of those things are important, what I have found is that many people neglect the very part of them that impacts both of those—our spirit, as the definition states above. I've known many people who have excellent physiques; they eat clean and they don't have any real illness to speak of, yet they never feel "well." I saw that a lot in the fitness industry. People would work out for many hours a day and literally weigh everything they put in their mouths but still not feel complete and healthy.

Even years later, when I was working in a functional medicine center, patients would try to get well with different supplements and medications based on various test results. We changed their diet and lifestyle, but *still,* some never truly got well. I've seen people go through recovery programs for different addictions, only to find themselves falling off months or years later back at square one. Behavior modification will only work for so long. Returning to the house metaphor (we can think of our being as a house), a good home starts with a good foundation. If the foundation is poor, the structure will be poor . . . no matter how good it may look on the outside. Houses, like our beings, need to be built on a firm foundation that is sturdy and strong.

The lifestyle of other cultures around the world directly oppose the culture here in the United States. Upon rising, many start the day with warm water and lemon or an herbal tea while spending quiet time in prayer and preparation for their day. Most Americans wake up to their coffee (a major stimulant that is rough on the nervous system—but I do love my coffee) or caffeine drink, turn on electronic devices, or rush off to the gym before work. In studying the cultural differences, we can see that there tend to be less disease, less stress, and a low obesity and morbidity rate, all because they slow down and implement intentional practices to pray and nurture their spirit.

We can look all around America and see just the opposite. We are probably one of the sickest and most obese nations on the globe. Can you see the difference? If you start your day with high stress and pressure, it will likely remain on that trajectory for the day. How do you start your day? If you're one of those folks in the majority in this country, maybe starting your day by nourishing your spirit first could contribute to added health benefits. We'll address stress in another chapter.

My health coaching practice looks completely different today than it did when I first started years ago. I thought food and exercise were the cure for everything. I thought if people would just clean up their diet and lifestyle habits and exercise more, they would be healthy. We know that those things are important, but the Bible clearly tells us in 1 Timothy 4:8 (NIV), "For physical training is of some value, but godliness has value for all things, holding promise for the present life and the life to come." I have concluded that it is impossible to experience true health and wellness without addressing our spirit first.

> **I HAVE CONCLUDED THAT IT IS IMPOSSIBLE TO EXPERIENCE TRUE HEALTH AND WELLNESS WITHOUT ADDRESSING OUR SPIRIT FIRST.**

God is a Spirit. John 4:24 (NIV) says, "God is spirit, and his worshipers must worship in the Spirit and in truth."

God created man in His own image. Genesis 1:27 (NIV) says, "So God created man in his own image, in the image of God he created him, male and female he created them."

Genesis 2:7 (NIV) says, "Then the LORD God formed a man from the dust of the ground and breathed into his nostrils the breath of life, and the man became a living being."

God is Spirit, and He made us in His image, so therefore, we are spirit.

> **IF WE HAVE A RELATIONSHIP WITH JESUS, WE HAVE THE POWER THROUGH HIM TO OVERCOME.**

Now that we've established that you are a spirit (in human form), what does it look like to nourish and take care of that part of you? It's important to know that God is pro-health! The Spirit must be the number one priority. I think a lot of people believe they must be "religious" or belong to some denomination. I've worked with many people over the years, and it wasn't until they uncovered something of a spiritual nature in themselves that they began to feel better overall. For example, unforgiveness could lead to a number of health-related issues, such as depression, anxiety, overeating, digestive issues, and even cancer.

I read a major study that found that patients at a cancer center who received forgiveness therapy recovered more quickly than patients who did not.[2] I'm not here to push a religion; I'm here to tell you the truth, and the truth is, until people come to the place

---

[2] Mary J. Hansen et al., "A Palliative Care Intervention in Forgiveness Therapy for Elderly Terminally Ill Cancer Patients," *Journal of Palliative Care* 25, no. 1 (2009): 51–60, https://doi.org/10.1177/https://doi.org/10.1177/082585970902500106.

where they believe that Jesus was sent by God the Father to be the sacrifice for sin (a revelation that all of mankind needs), make Him their Savior and Lord, and believe He rose from the dead and is alive today seated in heaven, their lives will be incomplete. We are lost without Jesus. He bought us at a very high price, and we owe it all to Him. That is the absolute cornerstone to overall health and wellness and the key to experiencing a balanced life. Does it mean we will never get sick? No. Does it mean we won't ever struggle? No. It means that if we have a relationship with Jesus, we have the power through Him to overcome. He gives us wisdom that no doctor, personal trainer, or financial advisor can give. He is the Giver of life and wisdom.

Why is wisdom so important? You might be thinking, *I just want to feel better. What does wisdom have to do with anything?* Or maybe you feel that you have enough wisdom but remain confused about why you're still stuck, still searching. I guess we need to distinguish between godly wisdom and worldly wisdom. We find this distinction in 1 Corinthians 3:19 (NIV): "For the wisdom of this world is foolishness in God's sight. As it is written: 'He catches the wise in their craftiness.'" So, maybe we aren't as smart as we think we are. God's wisdom is not man's wisdom, but God says He will give us wisdom if we ask. James 1:5–6 (NIV) says:

> *If any of you lacks wisdom, you should ask God, who gives generously to all without finding fault, and it will be given to you. But when you ask, you must believe and not doubt because the one who doubts is like a wave of the sea, blown and tossed by the wind.*

The book of Proverbs in the Bible is known as the book of wisdom, and Proverbs 24:14 (NIV) says, "Know also that wisdom is like honey for you: If you find it, there is a future hope for you, and your hope will not be cut off."

But we have to be alert because we have a real enemy who will do anything in his power to keep us from that wisdom, which should tell us something about how powerful God's wisdom is in leading us to a prosperous life. Jesus says in John 10:10 (NIV), "The thief comes only to steal and kill and destroy; I have come that they may have life and have it to the full." Who is the thief? That would be our enemy, the devil.

If you are a believer in Jesus and have made Him your Savior and Lord, then you have the Holy Spirit in you. God has given you His authority to use the name of Jesus (the name above every name) over everything that comes against you. That includes sickness, lack, depression, or anything that is not from Him. Luke 10:19 says, "Behold, I have given you authority to tread on serpents and scorpions, and over all the power of the enemy, and nothing shall hurt you." That is so powerful for those of us who have that personal relationship with Jesus. It's never about a religion; Jesus wasn't religious. In fact, He was always up against the religious rulers in His time on earth (the Pharisees). He was about a relationship and bringing people to God the Father. It's only through Him that our house of health and wellness can be built.

> **IT'S ONLY THROUGH JESUS THAT OUR HOUSE OF HEALTH AND WELLNESS CAN BE BUILT.**

This started making so much sense to me as the years went on. I began to understand why people still felt out of balance or unwell no matter how well they were eating, managing their stress, acquiring wealth, or exercising. The spiritual piece was missing. Let's unpack some key things that impact our spirit health.

OUR THOUGHTS

Thoughts are so powerful! They are one of the key contributors to nourishing our spirit. You've probably heard the saying (found in Proverbs 23:7), "For as he thinks in his heart, so *is* he" (NKJV). You become what you think about. I have worked with many people who have self-worth issues, typically rooted in some type of trauma they experienced in childhood—when we are the most impressionable. For example, if you had a parent, guardian, or someone significant in your life early on tell you that you were a mistake or the problem child or stupid or would never amount to anything, those words can fracture a child's self-worth. If a child wasn't protected by a parent or guardian or someone in authority as they should have been, that could lead them toward an unhealthy belief that they are worthless. I'll give you an example from my own life.

I was abused by a family member as a little child. When I finally exposed the abuser (which wasn't a topic of discussion back then like it is today), it didn't get handled properly, and I was left with this subconscious thought growing up that I must not be worth protecting, and something is wrong with me because "I" caused this upheaval and problem in my family. That thought lingered in my head for decades and led me to make some very poor choices in my life because, after all, in my mind, I wasn't worth much.

Nothing could have been further from the truth, and it wasn't until years later that I was able to reshape my thoughts by learning the truth about who God says I am and experience some inner healing. I had to renew my mind.

The Bible is clear in 2 Corinthians 10:5 when it tells us to "take captive every thought to make it obedient to Christ" (NIV). If you've never read that scripture before and are wondering what that means or how to take your thoughts captive, let me give you an example. Let's say someone's finances are creating a huge amount of stress and they keep thinking about it over and over until they become literally sick. The first step is to recognize they are rehearsing the destructive thoughts, and I believe we could all agree that does no good. Now, what does the Bible say about finances? If you don't read the Bible, you can simply change the narrative in your head to something like this: *I am working; I can make better choices with my money; I will get out of debt.* Encourage yourself and meditate on those statements instead. This practice will nourish your spirit and bring healing to your body (and finances).

> **IT'S VERY IMPORTANT TO KNOW WHAT GOD SAYS AND THEN TAKE INVENTORY OF OUR THOUGHTS AND BRING THEM INTO OBEDIENCE TO HIM.**

So, it's very important to know what God says and then take inventory of our thoughts and bring them into obedience to Him. Let me shift gears a little; let's think about it in terms of our health and wellness. If you're constantly ruminating on sickness, being overweight, or whatever health condition you are struggling with, then that will become your entire life and maybe even your identity. You'll start saying things like, "I'm depressed," "I'm fat," or "I'm broke." It will take over and manifest. How do you take those thoughts captive as 2 Corinthians 10:5 says? This is how I coach my clients: I tell them it's critical they know the truth because the truth is what God says about those self-critical statements.

To know the truth, you must go to His Word. Find verses that pertain and meditate on them. If it's a healing issue, you can look up multiple verses that have to do with healing and think on them (meditate on them). Watch how your life changes as you start to change your thinking—it's incredible. There are many podcasters out there today who are basically saying the same thing, except they leave out the biblical instruction. So, man knows that what they think about, they become. Here's a very powerful client example.

I started working with a beautiful woman whom I'll call Kathy. She loved Jesus, but she didn't love herself. She had made some very poor choices in her life (rooted in childhood trauma), which she continued to beat herself up over. When we first started working together, she referred to herself as "a loser." The first time I heard her say that, I stopped her. We can't expect good change to happen if our thoughts aren't in alignment with healing and wholeness. The first homework assignment I gave her was to meditate on who God says she is in the Scriptures. I'll talk more about her in a little bit.

What we meditate on truly does matter. Thoughts are a choice. I'm not saying to live in some fantasy land in your head, but we need to meditate on what we want that is good. Philippians 4:8 (NIV) tells us to think about "whatever is true, whatever is honorable, whatever is just, whatever is pure, whatever is lovely, whatever is commendable, if there is anything worthy of praise, think about these things." That's pretty clear, wouldn't you agree? Our bodies respond to how we think.

> **WHETHER YOU BELIEVE IN THE BIBLE OR NOT, YOU CAN LOOK UP ANYTHING IN LIFE, AND I GUARANTEE GOD HAS AN ANSWER FOR IT.**

It's been said that every cell in our bodies is impacted by the thoughts we think. To get what we want, we first need to think about it. If you want a relationship to improve, you first need to imagine what it would look like if it were better, not struggling. If you keep ruminating on the struggle, that's what you'll get. Even material objects were first created in someone's head. The chair you are sitting on was, at one point, just a thought in someone's head before it became a reality. We have the power to do that in our own lives. God gave us a brain and told us what to think about. Whether you believe in the Bible or not, you can look up anything in life, and I guarantee God has an answer for it. It's our blueprint for successful living. God took the guesswork out of everything. Proper thinking, in line with what God's Word says, will nourish our spirit man.

OUR WORDS

Just like our thoughts, the words we speak have a major impact on our spirit health. What we speak to ourselves, over our lives, and to others has tremendous outcomes. The Bible says, "The tongue has the power of life and death" (Proverbs 18:21, NIV). This was another major piece of wisdom and revelation that God gave me. But first, He needed to deal with me because I was the chief mumbler and complainer (ask my kids and husband!) I was constantly talking about the negative going on in my life. It was easy to discern how I was thinking because what you think about comes out of your mouth.

When you magnify anything, it gets bigger. God gave me a loving rebuke and course correction. He needed to teach me how important my words are because I was literally creating death with them. The Bible even says in James 3:10 (NIV), "Out of the same mouth come praise [blessing] and cursing. My brothers and sisters, this should not be." I felt like I got smacked by a ton of bricks because it hit home so hard. But I can honestly tell you that once you're thinking is right, your words will follow. When those two things are in alignment with what is good and acceptable, you then start operating in the power God tells us we have. The Bible says that God created everything with His words. Genesis 1:3 (NIV) says, "And God said, 'Let there be light,' and there was light." We can create life with our words, or we can create death with our words. If you walk by the mirror every day and say how fat you are or how much you hate your hair or whatever body part, your body hears you. Do you think it will be affected positively or negatively?

Instead, walk by and say, "I'm so grateful for [fill in the blank]." If you're working on weight loss, then praise or bless yourself for working on it. If you're working on saving money, then praise or bless yourself for the efforts you are making. If you are struggling in your marriage, then start speaking blessings over your spouse; start thinking about what it *will* look like when the relationship is restored. God restores, God heals, God redeems, and God will partner with you.

> **GOD RESTORES, GOD HEALS, GOD REDEEMS, AND GOD WILL PARTNER WITH YOU.**

Being aware of our spirit and taking good care of it through how we think and how we talk are critical changes we can make that will affect our overall health and well-being, just like we know eating right, exercising, sleeping, and minimizing stress keeps our body healthy. Just making these small changes creates huge potential for success. I've found, overall, that people who correct this first have more success than those who start with lifestyle changes.

My client, Kathy, whom I previously mentioned, needed to meditate on who God said she is. As Psalm 139:14 says, she is "fearfully and wonderfully made" (NIV). She needed to replace the old thoughts with the true thoughts. Then we worked on her words. Immediately I had her stop speaking the words "I'm a loser" over herself. She had been struggling to lose weight her whole life. Her weight became her identity. That, too, was false. She was trapped in a world of unforgiveness and hurt that was showing up in her physical health. I'm happy to report that today, she is walking in her power and authority, seeing herself the way God sees her, and most importantly, walking in her true identity, speaking and thinking differently about herself.

However, I have had some clients who reject this idea of nourishing their spirit. They are only driven by how they feel and how their body looks. I spent the early years of my coaching practice trying to touch "lightly" on spirit with people. Merely telling people to go out for a walk and connect with their Creator wasn't enough. I've learned that it is much deeper than that. I'm sad to say that those folks whom I have worked with over the years who are only bent on the physical aspect of healing end up chasing their health for years. Most of those people keep *saying* (words) how awful they feel, and the cycle just continues.

I know a gentleman who was chasing his health his whole life—always sick as a child and never feeling well as an adult. He went from doctor to doctor, spent enormous amounts of money on supplements, and more. He constantly complained (words) about how horrible he felt and would ruminate (thoughts) on it. He was basically addicted to what Google had to say about all his symptoms. Unfortunately, most doctors don't have the time it takes to do a proper intake with patients and ask them questions about past trauma and other things in their past that could be affecting their present. They don't tell you to change your words or change your thinking. Most people are left with the same problems they came in with, maybe prescribed a pill or supplement, and the root cause never gets addressed. Which leads me to the next point—the soul of a person.

TOXIC EMOTIONS

Toxic emotions such as bitterness, resentment, anger, and unforgiveness hurt our spirit and God's Spirit (Holy Spirit). These things have shown up time and time again when people are trying to heal from some physical ailment. Most organs in our bodies are connected to an emotion. For example, anger is connected to your liver. Most mental health issues are connected to your liver also. You can easily search for this on the Internet and find numerous articles on this.

I worked with a client some time ago. She believed in God but didn't really have a relationship with God. She had struggled with depression her entire adult life and was on medication, which obviously wasn't helping. We set out to get to the root cause of the depression by examining her sleep, her food, her stress, and much more. It wasn't until we got into the spiritual part of my 7-pillar coaching method that she had her "aha moment." She had been holding on to unforgiveness toward a family member for years. She came to that conclusion on her own without my prompting. It's such a blessing to witness people uncover these truths and then take hold of the power they have within them to cast away their victimhood and overcome it. I am happy to report that she was able to get off her psychoactive meds and switch over to a more natural supplement that supports her moods while walking through the forgiveness process.

> **WE COULD BE EXPERIENCING SO MUCH MORE OF THE ABUNDANT LIFE—THAT *SHALOM*—IF MORE PEOPLE WERE AWARE THAT THEIR SPIRIT NEEDS TO BE ADDRESSED BEFORE THE BODY.**

Sadly, our healthcare system isn't trained to work this way with people. They listen to symptoms and prescribe a treatment that only touches the body of a person. It's sad because we could be experiencing so much more of the abundant life—that *shalom*—if more people were aware that their spirit needs to be addressed before the body. Like I mentioned, past trauma, the thoughts we think, and the words we say play such a huge role in the way our body feels and reacts.

I hope that you can now see that you are a spirit with a temporal body. We have an obligation to take care of our body, but we can't do it the way we need to in order to create optimal health without examining our spirit first. As far as a relationship with Jesus goes, it's never too late. He's always there waiting for you. Romans 10:9 (NIV) says, "If you declare with your mouth, 'Jesus is Lord,' and believe in your heart that God raised him from the dead, you will be saved." That's when your relationship starts! If you just declared that . . . then welcome to the family! You are now a son or daughter of the most High God. You are royalty.

For those who do have that relationship with Him, maybe you need that reminder that your thoughts, words, and toxic emotions might be harming your spirit. Or maybe you were like me at one time, not understanding the power and authority God gave us as His followers to use against anything that comes against us. We know sickness and anything formed against us can't prosper, according to Isaiah 54:17. We are to put on our spiritual armor daily and stand against our adversary, the devil. He will rob us of everything we have if we let him.

> **IF OUR WORDS AND THOUGHTS LINE UP WITH GOD, THEN WE ARE SAFE.**

I'm not sure most people understand how real this adversary is and what his true agenda is. If God creates, the enemy destroys. If God is pro-health and life, the enemy wants to kill and make us sick and stuck. How does the enemy get access to any of us? He gains access through past trauma, the words we speak, the thoughts we think, and the things we watch, listen to, and participate in. If our words and thoughts line up with God, then we are safe. If we think and speak destructively and are involved in things that don't line up with what God would want for us, then we are fair game to the enemy. And just to be clear, the devil doesn't always look scary. The Bible says in 2 Corinthians 11:14 (NLT),

"But I am not surprised! Even Satan disguises himself as an angel of light."

Don't be deceived, the enemy can have us so focused on our bodies and health (which is good and important) that we divert our attention from our spirit health. I heard a preacher once say that the enemy's tactic is to deceive, distract, and destroy. I think we all see that there is a real enemy—just look around our world. Depravity is at an all-time high and is touching every facet of our lives. We fight a real battle, and that battle is light (God) versus darkness (Satan). Think of it like a football game; you're either on offense or defense. With God, we always have the ball. We always win with Him! But we give the enemy yardage by the way we talk, think, and act. If you mess up, then course correct, and pick up the ball and run with it.

Too many people cry out to God to rescue them, but God already has. He did everything He needed to do on the cross. He defeated every foe. And when He rose again, He made a spectacle of our enemy. He whooped every demon. When He returned to heaven and left us with His Holy Spirit, He also left us the name of Jesus and the authority of that name. We use that against anything that comes against us to steal, kill, and destroy. Remember Kathy? Well, when she understood how the enemy had been using her past trauma against her and she started walking in her power and authority to fight the spiritual battle against her spirit, her body, and her soul, she started walking in victory and experiencing breakthrough and change in her life.

> **YOU ARE NOT SUBJECT TO YOUR GENETIC DISPOSITION; YOU ARE NOT A VICTIM OF YOUR PAST, AND YOU ARE NOT HELPLESS. WE ARE ALWAYS VICTORIOUS, ALWAYS TRIUMPHANT, AND ALWAYS WITH HOPE.**

Get your thoughts in alignment with God's thoughts, use the words God uses, and watch your life change—that includes your health. You have power, authority, and dominion over all of it. Remember Luke 10:19 (NIV): "I have given you authority to trample on snakes and scorpions and to overcome all the power of the enemy; nothing will harm you." Wow!! You are not subject to your genetic disposition; you are not a victim of your past, and you are not helpless. We are always victorious, always triumphant, and always with hope.

PILLAR 2
NUTRITION

Now that the foundation has been laid, we can start building upon it. We can set up the structure that will lead to a balanced life and overall health and wellness. Let's put up the first wall of nutrition. I heard a cute joke recently: What did the one DNA strand say to the other DNA strand? . . . "Do these genes make me look fat?"

Here's the good news, you have control of your genes. I hear it all the time from clients that obesity runs in their families. Well, that isn't the case. What might be true, though, is that they learned some poor eating habits that got passed down through generations. We can control our genes. That's right! Straight from the CDC website:

> *Epigenetics is the study of how your behaviors and environment can cause changes that affect the way your genes work. Unlike genetic changes, epigenetic changes are reversible and do not change your DNA sequence, but they can change how your body reads a DNA sequence.*[3]

Isn't that amazing? No matter what your family history is, you can control your outcome. Powerful! God didn't leave us helpless.

---

[3] "What Is Epigenetics?" *Centers for Disease Control and Prevention*, 15 Aug. 2022, www.cdc.gov/genomics/disease/epigenetics.htm#:~:text=Epigenetics%20is%20the%20study%20of,body%20reads%20a%20DNA%20sequence.

He has given us so much freedom to choose—not just Him but how we take care of our bodies.

> **GOD DIDN'T LEAVE US HELPLESS. HE HAS GIVEN US SO MUCH FREEDOM TO CHOOSE—NOT JUST HIM BUT HOW WE TAKE CARE OF OUR BODIES.**

If you're one of the millions of Americans struggling to know what to eat, you're not alone. I don't mean what to make for dinner; I mean, literally, what is actually good for you? There are so many conflicting messages out there. You might be standing in a grocery checkout line staring at several magazines or scrolling social media, and one says that plant-based eating is the key to longevity and staving off illness, while something else says keto is the best way to burn fat by keeping your body in a state of ketosis, then yet another boasts savory carnivore type dishes telling us we need more protein. What is going on?

I don't know about you, but I've seen it all, tried it all, and had to come to my own conclusions. We have to understand that marketers and social media are profiting from and weaponizing our desperation to be well. There may be some truth to all of their claims, but figuring out what foods work for *your* body in the season of life that you're in may be easier than you think. Maybe you're familiar with the "My Plate" graphic. It basically breaks up five food groups (fruits, grains, proteins, and vegetables) into four almost equal quarters with dairy earning a small place on the side.[4] Or, maybe you remember the famous food pyramid. The Physicians Committee for Responsible Medicine came out with their version of the ideal (power) plate, which eliminates dairy and redefines "protein" to include legumes. Portion sizes are also different.[5] I urge you to look those up for yourself. A lot has changed in the nutrition world since those graphics were developed. To clear up any confusion, I'll offer some simple pointers that you can take away and start implementing right away into your diet later in this chapter.

First, I think it's important that we understand that food has one main purpose, and that is to nourish the body. When God made Adam and Eve in the Garden of Eden, He told them they could eat all the plants that were in the garden (all but that one specific tree). Genesis 1:29 says, "And God said, 'Behold, I have given you every plant yielding seed that is on the face of all the earth, and every tree with seed in its fruit. You shall have them for food.'" So, we can see that food serves a purpose; even Adam and Eve had to eat. One of the most famous quotes by Hippocrates is "Let food be thy medicine." That says it all. But if foods can nourish, fuel, and heal the body, we can conclude that foods could also hurt the body. I guess the big question is, how do *you* view food and what kind of relationship do *you* have with it? So many people I work with are often afraid to eat for fear of gaining weight or triggering some digestive disorder. Other people use food as comfort and others for entertainment.

---

[4] "My Plate," U.S. Department of Agriculture, accessed March 25, 2004, https://www.myplate.gov.
[5] Physicians Committee for Responsible Medicine, *ThePowerPlate.org*, https://p.widencdn.net/ktho8u/Power-Plate-Brochure.

While food can be all those things at different times, it's critical to have that solid understanding that we need to eat good food that nourishes and heals our bodies. Let's pick on sugar for a minute. No one needs to tell you that sugar is addictive and we need to minimize it daily. Why do you think it's one of the hardest habits to kick? Sugar hits your dopamine receptor in your brain (the reward/pleasure center) and makes you feel really good, but then has the backhanded effect of bringing on the crash. It will spike your blood sugar and make you crash quickly. When people are feeling down, depressed, anxious, or stressed, the body's natural pull is to feel good. That's where discipline (not willpower) needs to be developed. And trust me: no discipline = big consequences.

> **THAT'S WHERE DISCIPLINE (NOT WILLPOWER) NEEDS TO BE DEVELOPED. AND TRUST ME: NO DISCIPLINE = BIG CONSEQUENCES.**

I had a client who was going through major stress, and I mean major. She was working full time, her marriage was rocky, her husband was out of town a lot, and she had issues with her teen kids. She would come home from work, drink an entire bottle of wine, and eat a brick of cheese. Her body was screaming to feel good, and that's what she gravitated toward. Both alcohol and cheese have compounds that hit the pleasure center of the brain, are highly addictive, and have an assortment of negative effects on the body. Needless to say, she was struggling with depression and weight. She had no relationship with God of any kind. Her spirit was crushed and she was dealing with those symptoms. Proverbs 17:22 states, "A joyful heart is good medicine, but a crushed spirit dries up the bones." For this poor gal, it was very difficult for her to manage any of this on her own. Sadly, she only experienced minimal results. She gave in to the notion that it was just too much for her. She left her spirit health alone to deal with the physical but could not achieve lasting changes.

So, we know that sugar hurts us and is destructive to our health, but many other foods contribute as well, such as processed food and highly inflammatory foods. Processed foods that are loaded with chemicals and preservatives will do so much damage to your body, literally from head to toe. Some ingredients, like monosodium glutamate, actually make you crave more sugar. It's crazy! Brain function, moods, cellular function, and detoxification will suffer. The same goes for inflammatory foods (foods that produce inflammation in the body). Inflammation is the catalyst for almost all diseases, like arthritis, heart disease, joint pain, and even cancer. Here's a good rule to remember: if God made it, it's good for you, but if a factory made it, chances are, you have to really read labels and inspect it.

No one sets out to be addicted to anything. Let's look at the difference between willpower and discipline for a minute. Willpower is the motivation to exercise your will. Remember, your will is tied to your soul, which is your mind, will, and emotions. People may have plenty of motivation, but what if something is blocking the will, such as past trauma, wrong thinking, or poor habits formed around eating? I believe this is why so many people will join a gym to get fit and lose weight starting on January first of every new year, but within three months, they quickly get derailed and quit. If willpower is the motivation to exercise your will... how's that working out for you?

> **HERE'S A GOOD RULE TO REMEMBER: IF GOD MADE IT, IT'S GOOD FOR YOU, BUT IF A FACTORY MADE IT, CHANCES ARE, YOU HAVE TO REALLY READ LABELS AND INSPECT IT.**

This is why I prefer to think of wellness and getting healthy as a discipline. Not "getting disciplined" in the negative connotation, like punishment, but creating self–discipline. Creating a new discipline around food, fitness, stress, and elsewhere can set you up for success where you have more control over areas of your life versus trying to have the motivation to find the will to do something.

Having a strong "why" is what creates a discipline. For example, why do you pay your bills on time every month? Because you don't want debt collectors at your door. Why do you change the oil in your car regularly? Because you don't want to replace the engine. See the difference between willpower and discipline? Sometimes, discipline can be painful (maybe not always physically). You may feel like you're missing out when everyone at a family gathering is eating one way, and you know your body needs to eat another. I grew up hearing my father say that there are two types of pain: the pain of discipline and the pain of regret. You choose. You control the action because you want a certain outcome. That's part of the power we all have and need to be aware of. We need to recognize what's going on in our bodies when this happens and have strategies in place versus going on a quest for sugar or grabbing the first sugary thing that crosses our path.

Here are some disciplines that I have found helpful in refraining from grabbing the first thing in front of you to eat:

1) Make a decision to walk away from anything tempting.
2) Take a quick walk.
3) Implement a breathing technique for quick oxygen to your brain to get you into a relaxed state. Breathe in for four counts, hold for seven counts, and exhale for eight counts. Repeat three times. It truly works wonders, especially when we are stressed.

I've learned that the pain of regret is much worse than the pain of discipline. If you think that working out harder if you blew it over the weekend actually works—it doesn't. That mindset isn't a good discipline. Life will produce all kinds of tests and trials, and how we choose to manage them will be key to our health. In the following chapters, we'll see how addressing all those different areas can come into play and work together synergistically. We can do our part by making wise choices, but it's hard on our own. God is right there wanting to give us the wisdom and strength if we invite Him into our lives to do so.

Remember, in the previous chapter, we talked about God's wisdom versus our wisdom. Like we discussed in the last chapter, when people first develop a spiritual discipline of starting their day in quiet prayer time and meditating on God's Word, they set themselves up to create good disciplines in all the other areas of their lives. People rush through their day and just grab whatever food is around when they are hungry or stressed with no thought or preparation. You know the old saying, "People don't plan to fail; they just fail to plan"? Plan to have discipline when it comes to our food choices.

If you are a Christian, you most likely know these verses, "Or do you not know that your body is a temple of the Holy Spirit within you, whom you have from God? You are not your own, for you were bought with a price. So glorify God in your body" (1 Corinthians 6:19–20) or "So, whether you eat or drink, or whatever you do, do all to the glory of God" (1 Corinthians 10:31). Church gatherings are notorious for feeding us junk food. When I look around at the people at church, I see so many struggling with weight issues as well as other health issues. We need to develop discipline in ALL areas of our lives that will keep us healthy and in balance.

I worked with a gentleman who was dealing with a sluggish metabolism, wanting to lose weight even though he was working out all the time, but just couldn't figure out what was going on. This poor guy had no clue that Raisin Bran wasn't healthy for him because, for years, the marketing had been so clever in convincing us otherwise. When we did a grocery store tour, and I had him read the labels. He was shocked at what was in it—just the sugar alone, not to mention the other chemicals. That's how he started his day, either with a bowl of sugary cereal or a bagel, which is highly processed wheat and sugar. He was crashing by 10 a.m. and would go to the vending machine at work for a candy bar so he could get some quick energy. He kept spiking his blood sugar level and then crashing. This shuts down the metabolism when we aren't feeding it real food. Many people are doing the same thing.

However, when he started putting new disciplines in place, like food prepping and bringing his own snacks to work, he started seeing the changes he wanted. His workouts were better, and he was experiencing more energy. The body needs adequate amounts of protein, carbohydrates, and fat because they are macronutrients. But then, there is the ongoing debate on just how much protein, carbs, and fats we need (back to the marketing trap and expert opinions). The only opinion that matters is yours. You know how you feel, and you are the only one in control of what goes into your mouth.

> **THE ONLY OPINION THAT MATTERS IS YOURS. YOU KNOW HOW YOU FEEL, AND YOU ARE THE ONLY ONE IN CONTROL OF WHAT GOES INTO YOUR MOUTH.**

When I begin working with a new client, I have them keep a food journal. Some people love it, and others find it daunting, but almost all of them are happy that they do it because it uncovers so many clues as to what needs addressing. I tell them that there is no judgment coming from me and that transparency with themselves is key. I can't help uncover things if I don't know about them. If someone tells me they work out five days a week and eat really clean but need to lose twenty pounds, I scratch my head and think, well, there's something else going on in your body you need to see a doctor about, OR, you're eating something you're not disclosing. Keeping a food journal is very simple. You can simply document everything you put into your mouth (food and drink) and also include how much and at what time you are eating. The most frequently discovered patterns are portion control issues and eating far too close to bedtime. A staggering number of people are late-night snackers. When people get really honest with themselves and write down what they are actually eating, what's going on and how they can make adjustments usually becomes pretty clear. I have to say, food journaling is a great discipline.

FOODS THAT HEAL THE BODY

Now that we know how certain foods hurt the body, let's talk about foods that heal the body. In Matthew 4:4, Jesus told the devil, "It is written, 'Man shall not live by bread alone, but by every word that comes from the mouth of God.'" God's Word is the ultimate food for health and healing. That's why meditating on God's Word brings nourishment to our spirit and our body.

But in terms of actual food, probably the easiest example I can give about food that heals is soup. When people get sick with a cold or flu, what do they typically eat? For decades people have been making chicken soup . . . why is that? I believe that people instinctively know that broth is soothing to the gut; the warmth makes them feel good, and cut-up cooked veggies provide powerful nutrients that are needed to get the body well again. Think of the sickest you've ever been. Maybe you didn't even have an appetite, but if you did, I'm sure you weren't craving a Snickers bar. Our bodies are so smart that even when we are sick and out of balance, they know exactly what needs to heal. I'm not sure why people turn off those same listening ears they have when they get well again and go back to the foods that can hurt them. Do you see how poor discipline around your food choices can become a vicious cycle? Eating poorly creates sickness. Good nutritious foods build up the immune system, which protects against disease and sickness.

Let's go over the macronutrients, which are protein, carbohydrates, and fats. Just a disclaimer: I am in no way making suggestions or claims. I am just giving some clarity around the subject. But for the sake of the book, I want to address some key points. If you have certain medical conditions, you should seek a qualified healthcare practitioner who will help you navigate what's best for you.

PROTEIN

When people think of protein, they tend to think of animal meat. We've been trained that way. There have been subliminal and plain-as-day messaging that tell us that. We need to understand how the marketing industry works. They program us to think a certain way. I'm not trying to cause a fuss here, but it's the truth. You can look up numerous TED Talks where marketing companies talk about how they are hired to shape our minds into buying certain products and certain ideologies. Like I stated at the beginning of the book: I'm not here to push anything or say you shouldn't eat animal protein. Rather, I'm here to add to your knowledge.

The truth is, vegetables and legumes have great protein, and even some grains, like quinoa, are chock-full of it. The amount of protein that a person needs is based on a number of different factors, such as age, activity, and even certain health issues. Again, you should work with someone qualified who can help you navigate your specific needs. Just to give an example, a piece of red meat may contain 12 percent protein and iron, but it also contains inflammatory saturated fat. While spinach is made up of 29 percent protein, it has no fat and is loaded with iron and fiber. Maybe you are someone who needs to read that today.

Most people I work with are totally unaware of the benefits of cutting down on animal meat and eating more vegetables, legumes, and grains. In general, our population here in America isn't protein deficient but rather fiber and nutrient deficient. I will tell you that the factory-farmed animal industry is horrific. Animals are fed antibiotics due to the poor quality of their living environment in overcrowded pens that cause them to develop diseases. They are fed growth hormones to fatten them up. We end up ingesting all of that. When shopping for meat, I always recommend people find a local rancher that has cows, chickens, and turkeys and knows how they are raised and how they are finished. All of this is very important for our health.

On the contrary, maybe you're someone who doesn't like meat, and I work with folks like that all the time, so I reassure them that they can get plenty of complete protein by eating vegetables and grains. The food industry has changed so much over the years. Back in the day, we didn't have "organic" and "non-GMO" labels on things. We just went to the store and bought what we needed. Now you have to read every label. You have to know exactly what you're putting into your body. If you're interested in getting a free downloadable guide to plant-based living and free resources, you can visit my website.[6] Don't mistake eating plant-based for vegan—the base of what you are eating in a plant-based diet is plants—and so many plants contain an enormous amount of protein! You can still add high-quality animal protein should you desire.

CARBOHYDRATES

Carbs have become public enemy number one. There is such a huge misconception out there, and carbohydrates get lumped into one giant category. Some excellent carbs should be part of our diets. Many vegetables are mostly carbs, as are grains loaded with fiber. Yet people are terrified to eat carbohydrates simply because they don't know the difference. When we say "carb," most people think of pasta, bread, cakes, and potatoes. Your body processes and responds to each in vastly different ways. Traditional pasta is typically made of wheat. But more and more we are seeing quinoa pasta, brown rice pasta, egg pasta, and even legume-based pasta that contains no gluten, unlike wheat pasta. While you may not have celiac disease, you may experience gluten intolerance like most people. That's due to the process of genetically modifying wheat crops, mostly here in the US. Other countries, like Italy, don't have GMO crops. Nausea and bloating are frequent complaints from people with an intolerance to high amounts

---
[6] www.lorinolanhealth.com.

of gluten; those pastas I just mentioned may be a good replacement to try because they are filled with more fiber and even have protein, as well.

There are slow-digesting carbohydrates, like oats and grains, that keep your blood sugar level for longer periods of time than something like a piece of bread, sugary cereal, or cake—simple carbs that will spike your blood sugar level quickly. Simple carbs can be troublemakers because they quickly break down but will turn into fat if they aren't used up for energy right away. For example, if the 3 p.m. slump hits you while you're sitting at your desk at work, a simple carb may perk you up for a short time, but you will crash if you sit at your desk until 5 p.m. or later. This leaves you feeling tired again by dinner because you didn't go run around the block immediately after eating it. Instead, try eating some cut-up veggies and nuts with some hummus—good protein, good fats, and good carbs. The perfect afternoon pickup.

> **REMEMBER, IF GOD MADE IT, YOU'RE GOOD! IF A FACTORY MADE IT, USE CAUTION.**

I would encourage you to swap out the afternoon coffee, energy drink, or soda for some unsweetened green tea. Your body will thank you for it, I promise! On the other hand, if you have a more physically demanding job, you can get away with eating things like potatoes (a vegetable loaded with vitamins but a simple carb) that will give you some quick energy during the day. And, I feel like I need to say this: I said potatoes, not potato chips (wink, wink).

Just to recap: not all carbs are the enemy. By cutting them out, we may be depleting fiber, which is so necessary to keep our entire bodies cleaned up. Fiber is like little scrub brushes that clean out our digestive tract as well as our arteries and vessels. Aim to balance your diet between proper amounts of complex carbohydrates (specific to your needs) and balanced amounts of protein. Avoid those simple carbs—cakes, cookies, bars, packaged snacks, and the like—as much as possible. Remember, if God made it, you're good! If a factory made it, use caution.

FATS

The other macronutrient that is widely misunderstood is fat. Some people say to eat as much fat as you want, while others avoid it altogether. If you're old enough to remember the fat-free craze (maybe thirty-plus years ago), everything was fat-free. We were told that fat was bad, but canola oil and vegetable oil were good for you. Today we are learning that there is good fat and bad fat. Avocado oil and coconut oil have become popular also. The consumption of avocados, nuts, and seeds is on the rise. I do think that those types of oil, along with olive oil can be very good for you. The caveat is, when shopping for oil, be sure to look for organic, cold-pressed, non-refined, and hexane- and butane-free types. Oils that come in darker glass containers are preferable (no plastic) because they will keep them for longer periods of time. Basically, anything in a glass container is better for you than plastic because the chemicals in the plastic leach into the food, and the same goes for aluminum cans. The aluminum gets into the food.

When cooking with oils, we need to know which oils are best suited for what we are making. For example, most oils start to oxidize when they are at a high smoke point. Olive oil is particularly good for drizzling and light sauteing, but avocado oil and coconut oil have a much higher smoke point, meaning you can use them with higher-temperature cooking. When oils oxidize in your body, chemicals produce free radicals that can lead to sickness and disease. Always check your oil to know what it is best to cook with.

The blue zones of the world—five regions with the most people living to age one hundred years old or older—all have some basic things in common that contribute to their longevity, and one of those things is the way they eat. People in these blue zones have eaten what is thought to be the healthiest diet of all—the Mediterranean diet—for decades. These people consume healthy fats in small amounts, such as one to two handfuls of nuts and seeds per day in their high-quality oils. They eat some fish and meat less than five times a month. The basis of their diet is plant-based whole foods which are mostly vegetables and legumes (according to their food chart).[7] Fat consumption is personal, but having a well-balanced macronutrient plan for eating is key. The blue zone is probably the closest I have found to that and hope you check it out. They don't ignore fats; they just eat them in very healthy ways via nuts, seeds, and vegetables like avocados and proper oils. They don't consume high quantities of saturated fats that are found in meats.

---

[7] "Food Guidelines," *Blue Zones*, 27 July 2023, https://www.bluezones.com/recipes/food-guidelines/.

I want to include a few extra topics that seem to come up frequently when I am working with people on this nutrition pillar.

COFFEE

Coffee is one of the first questions I get from people. They always want to know if they can keep drinking it. There is much confusion around coffee. Not to be redundant, but that's marketing for you. My best advice is to limit your coffee to one to two cups in the morning. Anything past noon can disrupt sleep (even if you think it doesn't). We'll talk more about that in the sleep chapter. Next, only drink high-quality coffee. If you are a coffee lover like I am, then spend the money on it. Look for low-acidic organic brands that have been tested for mold and other impurities. Coffee beans are probably one of the biggest contributors to mold sickness. That's a real thing. So, making sure your coffee is high quality and knowing where the beans come from and how they are roasted is very important.

Coffee "brewing" has become so popular recently. Save yourself time and money, skip the drive-through, and make your own at home to be sure you are enjoying a quality cup of coffee. When you go to convenience stores or drive-throughs to get your coffee, you don't know what you're getting. The water they use may go through dirty lines filled with mold. And of course, sweetened creamers that are loaded with chemicals should be avoided and swapped out for a healthier version.

Another thing to consider with coffee is that it can be tough on the nervous system for some people. If you're someone who is struggling with anxiety, anger, or agitation, it may be best to limit or stay away from it completely, so your nervous system can heal and calm down. On the other hand, there are some surprising benefits to coffee, like lowering the risk of type 2 diabetes and increasing cardiovascular protection.

ALCOHOL

This is quite a taboo topic, especially in some Christian communities. You have people who are either pro-alcohol or anti-alcohol. The consumption of alcohol is a very personal decision based on many factors, including whether what the Bible has to say matters to you or not. The Bible does talk about alcohol specifically in multiple scriptures, but here are just a few to consider:

- "And do not get drunk with wine, for that is debauchery, but be filled with the Spirit." (Ephesians 5:18)
- "No longer drink only water, but use a little wine for the sake of your stomach and your frequent ailments." (1 Timothy 5:23)
- "It is good not to eat meat or drink wine or do anything that causes your brother to stumble." (Romans 14:21)

God tells us that misusing alcohol (getting drunk) is the problem. A little wine can be good for stomach ailments, but we need to consider if and when we are consuming it so that we do not cause someone else to stumble. Maybe you have been trying to stop or start a new habit, and a good friend becomes a stumbling block for you. For example, your friend may cause you to stumble if you're trying to give up sweets, but you feel pressured and give in when they want to stop for ice cream. I have plenty of friends who were really into the party scene and big-time drinkers before they gave their lives to Jesus. They no longer partake because for them, they don't want to cause themselves to stumble, let alone anyone else. If you've ever experienced getting drunk, it's not a good feeling to be out of your senses and out of control. People can make some life-altering choices when they are under the influence or filled with the spirit of drunkenness. But if you do enjoy alcohol on occasion, like anything else we consume, we need to make sure we are getting the best quality.

Let's take wine, for example. Like food, the labeling and oversight in the US are less strict than in many other European countries. Here in the US, we label anything that hasn't been sprayed or grown by a pesticide or herbicide with "organic." Places like Italy don't spray their grapes. The ingredient disclosure in the US tends to be less transparent than in other areas producing wine. Wine contains naturally occurring sulfites which gives some people headaches and congestion. The amount of sugar in wine will have some detrimental effects on your health as well, as does the actual alcohol content. Some producers of wine claim their grapes are all organic, farmed without water (meaning little to no mold), and contain no sugar and less alcohol. Worth looking into if you are a wine lover.

As far as hard liquor, again, this is a personal choice. At the very least, just make sure the quality is good and you know where it's coming from. Should you choose to partake in any alcohol-drinking, limit it to support your overall health and wellness. Alcohol can impair brain function as well as liver detoxification. I've worked with many women who love their white wine, which is made from grapes that are higher in sugar content compared to red wine, and then they wonder why they can't lose weight. I've read some studies that say women can consume five glasses of wine (5 oz.) per week or 2 oz. of liquor, while men can handle double those numbers. One meta-analysis found that wine is a leading contributor to breast cancer in women.[8] But to be fair, many things contribute to cancer—I do not want to pick on just alcohol. We also can't forget that lifestyle can change gene expression, which causes cancer genes to turn on or off. If you have a chance to check out the blue zones I just mentioned earlier, you will see moderate wine consumption is part of their habits.

> **WE ALSO CAN'T FORGET THAT LIFESTYLE CAN CHANGE GENE EXPRESSION, WHICH CAUSES CANCER GENES TO TURN ON OR OFF.**

INTERMITTENT FASTING

To fast or not to fast, that's the question that I get quite often. Another hot topic that has emerged over the past decade or so. There are many ways to fast, and people should fast in a way that works for them. Many health conditions restrict the ability to fast. I believe the easiest and safest way for most people is a twelve-hour window from dinner to breakfast while you are sleeping. The word breakfast is BREAK FAST. So if you eat dinner between 6 and 7 p.m., don't eat breakfast until 6 or 7 a.m. Simple!

---

8 Jasmine A. McDonald et al., "Alcohol Intake and Breast Cancer Risk: Weighing the Overall Evidence," Current Breast Cancer Report 5, no. 3 (Sept. 2013): 208–221, https://doi.org/10.1007/s12609-013-0114-z.

REMEMBER, YOU KNOW YOU BEST!

There are many benefits to fasting, and some experts say the longer you fast, the better. Fasting is even biblical but isn't always about food. Here we're speaking about a food fast for cell recovery and for your body to rest and digest what it's been fed throughout the day to keep it going. If you've consumed an adequate amount of good protein, carbs, and fats throughout the day, chances are, you are ready to shut the factory down (your body) and get ready to sleep, refresh, and recover. Every time you give your body food (fuel) it turns on, processes it, and uses it to work, putting out energy. You don't need to do that in the middle of the night.

Make sure dinner is a high-protein meal to ensure a good night's sleep. When people eat too close to bedtime, they open the factory back up, and every organ and cell has to go to work again. There should be a two- to three-hour window between dinner and bedtime for digestion. There are plenty of good articles and books out there on the art of fasting, and you can trial and error what works best for you, but know that you need at least a twelve-hour fast to give your body a chance to rest and clean up. Intermittent fasting not only removes damaged cells but also allows healthy cells nearby to get the nutrients and oxygen they need to start the healing and recovery process. Regeneration of cellular components is also possible, especially when it comes to mitochondria and other vital elements.

My hope is that you now feel empowered and encouraged with greater clarity on things that may have been confusing before. There is so much information out there that can get overwhelming. Dispelling myths is always powerful. I hope you got some nuggets of truth and ideas on how you can start implementing better eating habits. Remember, you know you best! We all go through different seasons of life, and sometimes we need to change things up and explore new options versus taking the same path and getting the same results that no longer serve us. Start thinking about the new disciplines you can put into place. Food is the best medicine, but please seek medical advice when necessary if you have a medical condition.

PILLAR 3

STRESS

Can I tell you that I have been stressing out about writing this chapter? I'm not sure why, but I've been getting pretty worked up over it. Quite frankly, writing this entire book has created a bit of stress for me, so I wanted to use it as an example right out of the gate. Typically, when we think about stress, we think about the negative type of stress that is often referred to as distress. When this type of stress is chronic and ongoing, it can be very destructive to our lives and our health. But have you ever heard of eustress pronounced *yoo-stress*? This type of stress can positively impact our health. Let's start with eustress so that later when we discuss taking inventory of our daily lives, we can put things in their proper category of either eustress or distress.

> **HAVE YOU EVER HEARD OF EUSTRESS PRONOUNCED *YOO-STRESS*? THIS TYPE OF STRESS CAN POSITIVELY IMPACT OUR HEALTH.**

So how can eustress be good for us? The stress I am under in writing this book is good stress. It is causing excitement and motivation and giving me a sense of urgency to complete a task. Short bouts of this type of stress are very good. Eustress is how we grow constructively and maximize productivity. Some other examples would be working out, training for a sport, starting a new job or a new relationship, or even building a new home. Maybe this is the first time you've heard that word, or maybe it's the first time you've heard that stress could actually be good for you.

I think it's really important to look at the situations or people in your life and determine whether they are a source of eustress or distress because, remember, not all stress is negative; some stress may be positive for you. You may be lumping all stress as bad or negative. Here's an example. Say you are single, start dating someone, and begin navigating the growing pains of having this new person in your life. You will have to grow with the other person—they bring in their baggage, you bring in yours, and then you start to see where it will go. Would you call that a positive or negative stressor? It could be either, depending on the baggage. The new relationship would fall into the distress category if there is toxicity or unhealthy dynamics. On the other hand, even though all relationships require a great deal of work to navigate stressors, your relationship would fall into the eustress category if you approach it as an opportunity to grow as an individual and as a unit. Be sure to take these inventories in your life so that you don't classify every stress as negative. Some are good for us, and we need to embrace them in order to grow and learn.

Let's flip the coin and talk about distress STRESS—the type that can be dangerous if it becomes chronic and unattended. This type of stress is more destructive and negatively impacts us. I'm sure you've all experienced this type of stress at some point. Maybe you lost a job, finances, a loved one, a home, have had an illness, or are experiencing ongoing strife and struggle in a relationship. Our bodies need serious support for these stressors. It's critical to protect our health, including our mental health. Managing stress has been a very hot topic for decades. The internet is loaded with articles about it, and bookstore shelves are filled with ways to manage it. I understand—sometimes it can feel impossible to manage stress. But just like with our food, we need to create certain disciplines and implement them if we are going to effectively manage these types of things that cause distress in our lives.

> **MY GO-TO RESOURCE FOR EVERYTHING IN LIFE IS THE BIBLE. GOD'S WORD. HE KNOWS IT ALL, CREATED IT ALL, AND HAS SOMETHING TO SAY ABOUT IT ALL.**

My go-to resource for everything in life is the Bible. God's Word. He knows it all, created it all, and has something to say about it all. Probably the one verse that people go to when they are feeling stressed or anxious is Philippians 4:6, "Do not be anxious about anything, but in everything by prayer and supplication, with thanksgiving let your requests be made known unto God." So right there, we have an open invitation from God to go to Him in prayer and talk about those things that are making us anxious.

It gets better as we go on to verse 7, which says, "and the peace of God, which surpasses all understanding, will guard your hearts and minds through Christ Jesus." Right there we see that by taking our stress to God and giving Him all our worries and concerns, He tells us He will give us His peace that will guard our hearts and our minds—think protection for heart disease and high blood pressure, think protection from depression and anxiety.

God tells us not to stress or be anxious about literally anything. He tells us to pray and be thankful, and then He will give us that peace (which leads to health). I don't know about you, but I find that amazing! Let's look at how stress can negatively impact our bodies if we don't address it, and then we will look at ways to support the body during times of great distress using food and lifestyle.

Here is a non-exhaustive list of possible side effects of stress on the body.

PHYSICAL STRESSOR	EFFECT ON THE BODY
Headaches	Increased depression and anxiety
Heartburn	Insomnia
Rapid breathing	Weakened immune system
Risk of heart attack/ high blood pressure	High blood sugar
Pounding heart	High cholesterol
Fertility Issues	Increased cortisol Stomachache Hair loss
Erectile dysfunction	Low sex drive
Missed periods	Tense muscles/pain

Stress is a natural physical and mental reaction to the things we experience in life. If you are dealing with anything listed above, you may have some stress that needs addressing. You can see that negative stress can impact every system of the body. Stress is that silent killer, and a lot of times, we start looking at other things as the culprit when really, underlying stress is the cause. I was working with a seventy-year-old woman back in 2021. Her doctor (whom I knew quite well) sent her to me because she had high cholesterol and didn't want to go on a drug for it. He knew that if she changed her diet, her cholesterol could decrease without medication, so he referred her to me.

She was a lovely woman, very well educated, a college professor, a writer, and loved running. We had been working together for several months, going through her food and her activity level. We did change a few things in her diet but not much because she was eating well and was actually *losing* weight (which does happen on occasion when under stress, depending on a person's metabolism). Regardless, this was a bit perplexing to me. But then she started opening up about her stress levels. We were on the heels of the pandemic from 2020, where she spent most of her time indoors and secluded out of fear. Remember those days?? It was a horrible time, and many people suffered terrible depression and anxiety over the whole thing. I don't even like to recall it. But we can learn and grow, even from the most stressful times.

We discovered that her stress was causing her cholesterol to be elevated. It wasn't coming from her diet. After we uncovered it, she went to work on putting new strategies in place, which I will discuss below. We worked together for six months, and when she went back to the doctor, her cholesterol had dropped eighty-six points. As if that enough wasn't great news, she then sent me a photo of her and her daughter finishing a race together. The stress and fear were gone. She was healthy and thriving. I know we have come to believe that our diet is the only thing that controls things like cholesterol, but we know better now—stress can impact it and other health markers, also. Just to point out, even though diet wasn't necessarily the cause of her cholesterol spike here, I want to mention that food can definitely be a major contributor to stress. As I mentioned back in chapter 2, food plays an important physiological role in our body's response. Eating processed foods laced with all types of chemicals, additives, and colorings will absolutely affect how your brain fires. Neurotoxins can even be found in food, skincare, makeup and cleaning supplies.

THE GUT IS BRAIN #2.

I know it's sometimes easier to try and tackle the things we feel we can control, like our food choices. Maybe your stress seems unmanageable and intimidating, and that's why it gets overlooked with certain medical conditions. When I worked in functional medicine, one of the first things we did with kids and adults with anxiety, depression, and other mental health issues was remove certain foods they were eating. This allows the brain to start firing properly, and more importantly, the gut starts to repair, which is critical for mental health. The gut is brain #2. You may have heard that there is a gut–brain axis. It is because of this gut–brain axis that you may feel nauseous or have no appetite when you are nervous or under stress. It's all connected. Feeding the body with proper nutrition that can actually help support and/or stave off stress repercussions in the body is so important.

Let's start with foods that help stress before we dive into lifestyle habits.

FOODS THAT SUPPORT THE BODY IN TIMES OF NEGATIVE STRESS

Remember the Hippocrates quote, "Let food be thy medicine"? There are many foods that we should be consuming, especially in times of stress, when the body gets depleted of necessary nutrients. When we get stressed, typically, we want a quick dopamine hit to the brain, something sugary, or a simple processed carbohydrate that will release energy quickly. Unfortunately, that doesn't nourish the body and will actually have the opposite effect. That's why being intentional, educated, and disciplined with food when stressed can make all the difference and heal the brain and body.

1) Dark leafy greens contain high levels of magnesium, which has been known to calm the body. We can take magnesium safely during the day and again in the evening, when stress may rob us of good quality sleep. But simply adding more dark leafy greens in addition to supplementation will help.

2) Chia seeds are another great source of magnesium. They also contain high levels of Omega-3 fatty acids, which provide anti–inflammatory benefits to all parts of the body. Many doctors and researchers are beginning to learn that the epidemic of depression and anxiety has a lot to do with diet and a deficiency in Omega-3.

3) Avocados are loaded with B vitamins, which support healthy nerves. It also supports healthy brain cells. They are another vitamin source that has been linked to depression and anxiety when deficient.

4) Nuts, such as almonds, cashews, and walnuts, all contain zinc. Zinc is very important in the body because it regulates its response to stress. Zinc is also critical to immune function. Nuts also contain magnesium.

5) Dark chocolate is a treat that everyone loves! I sometimes tell my clients to suck on a small piece of dark chocolate at night, especially if they tend to have a sweet craving. It's not only packed with antioxidants, but it's also another great source of magnesium. Dark chocolate (70 percent cacao) will boost your mood and have polyphenols which can reduce stress.

6) Green tea is an easy swap for the afternoon coffee. It not only has less caffeine but epigallocatechin gallate (EGCG) which helps reduce stress, prevents cancer, and contains an amino acid theanine which promotes relaxation.

7) Beans have high levels of folate, a B vitamin that has been shown to reduce stress and regulate mood. They also contain B-6 which helps prevent fatigue that can normally happen when under stress.

You can read up on these foods on the NIH's NCBI page[9] or find empirical research in their library search engine.[10]

If you live in the United States, as I do, I think we can all agree that we've been marketed to think that bigger and more is better (I could even say that we have been brainwashed to think this

---

9   *National Center for Biotechnology Information*, U.S. National Library of Medicine, www.ncbi.nlm.nih.gov/.
10   "PubMed," *National Center for Biotechnology Information*, U.S. National Library of Medicine, pubmed.ncbi.nlm.nih.gov/.

way). We are probably one of, if not *the only* country, with the highest obesity and mortality rates, and I tend to think it is due to the amount of stress we are under and the food we eat. Other countries eat smaller meals that are healthier.

Remember the blue zones that we talked about in the last chapter? Notice how all the foods I just mentioned are part of their daily diets. They live to be one hundred years or older because they are happier and healthier by consuming foods that bring health to their bodies. Managing our stress and eating properly is preventive medicine. When was the last time your doctor talked to you about that? We need to be our own advocates when it comes to our health. Continual learning and researching empower us to make educated decisions with our bodies. For far too long, we have given that control over to the medical professionals who don't have the time to listen to us, and most don't have the training to help us, other than to prescribe medication. I'm not picking on doctors. It's not their fault. They are simply operating according to the system they are trained in.

> **MANAGING OUR STRESS AND EATING PROPERLY IS PREVENTIVE MEDICINE.**

LIFESTYLE PRACTICES FOR MITIGATING NEGATIVE STRESS

I just want to note here that starting small and making one change at a time can have huge benefits. Most people aren't ready to dive into the deep end and make too many changes. If that's you, that's okay. Take one or two things and start integrating them into your daily practices, and see how they work. Here are some of the best techniques that have worked really well for my clients:

Read the Bible

Use His affirming words when you speak. In chapter 1, we talked about our spirit and the power of our words. When we continue to speak negative words and phrases over our situations, they tend to grow and get bigger, creating more stress. When we change our words, our bodies relax. As this becomes a lifestyle, our bodies will no longer respond to negative words in the same way. For example, if someone is having financial issues but all they talk about is their financial issues, the cycle will persist. Things like "We're so broke," "We are drowning in debt," or "We just can't afford it" feed the stress. We have to swap these statements out for verbiage like, "Right now, it's not in our budget" or "We are working on reducing our debt." Make your negative words positive. Our bodies hear us and feel the stress we feel. There are well over one hundred verses that have to do with stress, worry, and anxiety, but here are some good ones to begin meditating on and speaking out loud.

- John 14:27: "Peace I leave with you; my peace I give to you. Not as the world gives do I give to you. Let not your hearts be troubled, neither let them be afraid."
- Psalm 55:22: "Cast your burden on the LORD, and he will sustain you; he will never permit the righteous to be moved."

- Psalm 118:5–6: "Out of my distress I called on the LORD; the LORD answered me and set me free. The LORD is on my side; I will not fear. What can man do to me?"
- Proverbs 12:25: "Anxiety in a man's heart weighs him down, but a good word makes him glad."
- Matthew 11:28–30: "Come to me, all who labor and are heavy laden, and I will give you rest. Take my yoke upon you, and learn from me, for I am gentle and lowly in heart, and you will find rest for your souls. For my yoke is easy, and my burden is light."
- Romans 8:31: "What then shall we say to these things? If God is for us, who can be against us?"
- Romans 8:28: "And we know that for those who love God all things work together for good, for those who are called according to his purpose."
- Matthew 6:34: "Therefore do not be anxious about tomorrow, for tomorrow will be anxious for itself. Sufficient for the day is its own trouble."
- Matthew 6:27: "And which of you by being anxious can add a single hour to his span of life?"
- James 1:12: "Blessed is the man who remains steadfast under trial, for when he has stood the test he will receive the crown of life, which God has promised to those who love him."
- Philippians 4:6–7: "Do not be anxious about anything, but in everything by prayer and supplication with thanksgiving let your requests be made known to God. And the peace of God, which surpasses all understanding, will guard your hearts and your minds in Christ Jesus."

WE CAN SHIFT OUR ENVIRONMENT BY OUR WORDS.

Let me share a quick story of a woman I worked with. She had battled fear, stress, and anxiety all her adult life. She was a strong believer in Christ but did not know how using words could change her situation. When I say situation, I'm not necessarily referring to the literal situation, but it changed *her* until the actual situation changed. We can shift our environment by our words. Now don't get freaked out—hear me out. When this woman kept reacting out of stress and fear, which was typically through anger (because anger is just a secondary emotion to a deeper root problem, in this case, the stress and fear), her environment became more toxic. She was adding more stress to her body and the people around her. When she began to speak God's Word into things that were causing her fear and stress, everything began to change. We started with 2 Timothy 1:7 (NKJV), "For God did not give us a spirit of fear, but of power and of love and of a sound mind." The more she spoke it, the more the fear dissipated. Fear = stress. God doesn't give us fear. As a matter of fact, he tells us not to fear 366 times in the Bible; that's one reminder for each day and one for good measure.

Talking to God through prayer is relaxing to the spirit and soul. Bringing our requests to God who can handle them brings peace and comfort. When you find yourself "stressing out," pause and pray. Easy to remember, right? Pause and pray! If you're a prayer warrior, then I hope this is just a little reminder. But if you are someone who doesn't really pray and is unsure of what that looks like, here is a suggestion: it doesn't have to be full of big biblical words. It's quite literally talking to God. You might say, "Dear God, I need your help with the stress I am under. I can't do this on my own. Thank you, in Jesus's name, Amen." Why do we close prayer that way? Because John 14:13–14 (NKJV) says, "And whatever you ask in My name, that I will do, that the Father may be glorified in the Son. If you ask anything in My name, I will do *it*."

Rest

A lot of people, me included, have a hard time resting. What does rest look like for you? I tend to have two speeds: fast and off. If you are like me, we need discipline to make sure our bodies get rest. This includes good quality sleep, which we will talk about in the next chapter, but for right now, I want to address the go–getters and high achievers who run hard, play hard, and experience burnout due to high levels of stress. Taking walks, short naps, and just tuning out the noise can have tremendous health benefits. Put on some relaxing music and just take some time to rest. In countries like Italy and Spain, some regions shut down their commerce for an hour or so during the day, so the workers can nap and rest. Oftentimes, our minds can't shut down, so we need to train them just like you train our bodies with weights or running. Put away all devices for a short time and just be still.

Recall Philippians 4:6–7 where God tells us not to be anxious. In verses 4:8–9 (NKJV), He tells us what to think about:

Finally, brethren, whatever things are *true, whatever things* are *noble, whatever things* are *just, whatever things* are *pure, whatever things* are *lovely, whatever things* are *of good report, if* there is *any virtue and if* there is *anything praiseworthy—meditate on these things. The things which you learned and received and heard and saw in me, these do, and the God of peace will be with you.*

Sometimes, I even struggle to find a replacement for what I am thinking and feeling. How do I replace some of my most needling thoughts with what is true, right, and noble? If I look in the mirror and say, "I am so overwhelmed and stressed all the time," I could replace it with a true statement like, "I am taking one step at a time, working toward my goals."

Keep a Journal

Writing down our thoughts and feelings during times of stress can be very therapeutic. Stuffing our stress and pretending like we have it all together can be really dangerous. It will come out eventually, either physiologically or on other people. That's why writing it out not only helps you get it out but helps you process it.

Exercise

We will talk more about exercise in chapter 5. Studies have shown that exercise can have immediate benefits, such as bringing oxygen to your brain to improve brain function and protect your memory. Stress can make us feel confused and brain foggy. Eventually, exercise will lower blood pressure and protect your heart as well.

Breathing Techniques

Doing an easy technique like 4–7–8 will also bring instant stress relief and oxygen to your brain. Breathe in through your nose for a count of four, hold for seven, and then blow out your mouth for eight counts. Do no more than three sets (or you might feel a little woozy), but a few rounds will help you feel more calm and clear. You may find you will have to do this several times throughout the day if you are getting stressed—just to get your body regulated.

Boundaries

Some people have a hard time with boundaries for many reasons. They may not understand what it means to set boundaries. Many Christians may fear that boundaries would be unloving towards another person.

Let's say you are working forty-plus hours a week, feeling burnt out (you could be a stay-at-home mom), and have volunteer projects or serving opportunities on the weekends or after work. This could be a warning sign that you need a boundary. It is okay to say no to some things. If you tend to be a "yes person" who can't turn people down if they ask for help, you need to set up a healthy boundary to help alleviate your stress load. Only you can do that. Saying yes to worthwhile causes is wonderful, but if it starts to cost you family time and your own peace, then it's time to start learning to say no to some things—even if it's just for a short time, so you can rest and regroup.

Let's examine boundaries within the context of a relationship with a friend, coworker, or even a family member. Maybe the person is just negative and emotionally draining you. Emotional vampires are real, and they tend to suck the life out of people who will let them. You can still be loving and set up a healthy boundary with these types of people by either limiting your time or simply being honest with them. It's as simple as, "I care about what is going on with you, but perhaps finding someone else to talk to would be a good idea because I am working through my own stress."

If it's a toxic coworker, do what you can to limit time with that person. If that's impossible, ask to be reassigned away from them or quite literally leave the environment. I've had two jobs in my life that were horrendously stressful. In one, I was "used" to grow a business. The owners had no concern for me whatsoever while I was overloaded and stressed out on their behalf. The other was a completely toxic environment of stress from the doctor all the way down to the office staff. The only option for me was to resign. Only you can guard your heart like the Bible says, and to me, that sounds like putting up healthy boundaries so that others cannot steal your peace.

Make Time for Fun

Fun is the best remedy when we feel stressed, and I think we can all agree that a good laugh and fun times make us feel good. It's part of balancing your life. We can't work, work, work all the time. We need to incorporate a time of rest, fun, and laughter. Proverbs 17:22 says, "A joyful heart is good medicine, but a crushed spirit dries up the bones." Stress can crush us, and as we have read, it can lead to disease and illness, which dry up our bones. If God Himself tells us to have a joyful heart, we should listen. Our purest joy comes from Him, but I'm sure He would encourage some fun outside of Him.

> **IF GOD HIMSELF TELLS US TO HAVE A JOYFUL HEART, WE SHOULD LISTEN.**

I hope you have a better understanding of the different types of stress. I hope you see all the wonderful things God has to say about it in the Bible because I believe He knew how stressed we would be living in this world. He never leaves us guessing or struggling on our own. Besides meditating on that wonderful truth alone, you can start today by going through the same process I use with my clients. Write down all the things that are creating stress in your life. Assess each one to see if it is either constructive and motivating (eustress) or destructive and draining (distress). You may be pleasantly surprised to find that not all your stress is bad. You may even find that it is helping you to grow! Knowledge is power. It is your key to success.

PILLAR 4

SLEEP

The next wall is going up, and it's very important. Sleep deprivation is becoming a huge epidemic all over the world. Every day, millions of people decide to give up sleep for something else. There's a really old saying (which I've never liked because it's totally untrue) that says, "Oh, I'll sleep when I'm dead." If you're a Christian, you know that when you die, you will not be sleeping. I guarantee it! There's this crazy misconception that we can give up some sleep and still function and be healthy. It's absurd. Sleeping is critical to our health in so many ways. Just like eating, sleeping is natural. Our bodies crave food for energy, and our bodies crave sleep for rest and rejuvenation. Though a crazy example, think of it like an update for your phone. When you let it update, your phone runs faster and more efficiently. I have an Android and will get alerts that my phone wants to update. If I keep delaying the update, eventually, my phone will do it on its own. Your body is the same way. If you keep denying it proper sleep, it will eventually shut down and make you sick. Your body will then *force* you to sleep and rest.

> **IF YOU KEEP DENYING YOUR BODY PROPER SLEEP, IT WILL EVENTUALLY SHUT DOWN AND MAKE YOU SICK. IT WILL THEN FORCE YOU TO SLEEP AND REST.**

Our bodies were designed to rest, recover, and repair during the hours after the sun goes down. Of course, the Bible has a lot to say about sleep. Let's look at a few verses. Jeremiah 31:25–26 says, "For I will satisfy the weary soul, and every languishing soul I will replenish. At this I awoke and looked, and my sleep was pleasant to me." First Thessalonians 5:7 states, "For those who sleep, sleep at night." Exodus 33:14 finishes with, "And he said, 'My presence will go with you, and I will give you rest.'" I believe God designed us to sleep for a reason. It *is* good for our bodies, and we *feel* good after a good night's sleep. Proper restorative sleep can be the difference maker in life between "just making it through the day" and an energy-filled day that makes you feel accomplished and productive.

Perhaps you've heard of the concept of circadian rhythms. These are twenty-four-hour cycles that are part of the body's internal clock. They run in the background and carry out different functions. One of them is our sleep cycle. We have an internal "clock," and it gets influenced by our environment, especially light—this is why circadian rhythms are tied to the sun coming up and the sun going down. Most people's bodies know that when the sun comes up, it's time to get up and get our day started. We feel energized if we've had a good night of restorative sleep. Later in the day, when the sun is going down, there is less light, and it becomes dark, we are relaxed, winding down, and getting more tired and ready to sleep. When this circadian rhythm is thrown off, it causes the body's systems to not function optimally.

As I've mentioned before, if you are having severe issues with sleep, you may want to have a sleep study done by a qualified practitioner. This chapter will uncover insights for the rest of those who want to know more about sleep, how to get to sleep, and how to stay asleep. I will talk about things that hamper our sleep and ways to implement good sleep hygiene. Developing a nightly hygiene routine is just as important as a morning routine that goes beyond brushing our teeth and washing our faces. Also, we will look at how some foods, herbs, and other techniques can help you sleep better and for longer.

First, let's talk about what an "adequate" amount of sleep is for a normal adult. I know there are rare breeds who function on only four to five hours per night, but studies have shown over and over that adults need a solid seven to nine hours per night with one and a half to two hours of deep sleep within that seven – to nine-hour window. According to Healthline, the CDC states that 25 percent of sleep should be deep sleep.[11] All sleep is important, but REM sleep in particular plays a vital role in dreaming, memory, emotional processing, and healthy brain development.

- Dreaming: A majority of your dreams take place during REM sleep. However, REM is not the only stage in which dreams occur—that's actually a common myth about sleep.

---
11   CDC advisement, quoted in "How Much Deep, Light, and REM Sleep Do You Need?" *Healthline*, https://www.healthline.com/health/how-much-deep-sleep-do-you-need#takeaway.

That said, the dreams you experience in REM sleep are usually more vivid than non-REM sleep dreams.
- Emotional Processing: Your brain processes emotions during REM sleep. Dreams, which are more vivid in REM sleep, may be involved in emotional processing. Also, your amygdala, the part of your brain that processes emotions, activates during REM sleep.
- Memory Consolidation: During REM sleep, your brain processes new learnings and motor skills from the day, committing some to memory, maintaining others, and deciding which ones to delete. Some memory consolidation also takes place in deep sleep.
- Brain Development: Researchers hypothesize REM sleep promotes brain development since newborns spend most of their sleep time in REM. Adding to the evidence is that animals born with less developed brains, such as humans and puppies, spend even more time in REM sleep during infancy than those that are born with more developed brains, like horses and birds.

Wakefulness Preparation: REM sleep, through its activation of our central nervous system, might help us get ready to wake back up. This may explain why we spend increasing amounts of time in REM sleep as the night progresses and why we are easier to wake up during this stage.[12]

People go through two types of sleep in each sleep cycle: one stage of rapid eye movement (REM) and three stages of non–rapid eye movement (NREM). NREM is further divided into

---

12   Jay Summer and Dr. Abhinav Singh, "REM Sleep: What It Is and Why It's Important," *Sleep Foundation*, 22 March 2024, https://www.sleepfoundation.org/stages-of-sleep/rem-sleep.

three stages: light (N1), deep (N2), deeper (N3). A person cycles through these stages between four to five times every night in this order: N1, N2, N3, N2, REM. Each cycle lasts around ninety to 110 minutes. The first REM stage is short but becomes longer than NREM as sleep progresses.

How much deep sleep should we get? In healthy adults, about 70 percent of sleep is deep sleep and around 25 percent of your sleeping time is your deepest sleep. So, if you sleep between seven and eight hours, the time spent in your deepest sleep should be around 105–120 minutes or one and three-quarters to two hours. However, as you get older, you'll need less of this very deep sleep and spend more time in N2. During the deepest sleep, a variety of functions take place, including:

- Relaxation of muscles
- Increased blood supply to the muscles
- Slowed heart rate and breathing
- Tissue growth and repair
- Release of essential hormones

Without deep sleep, these functions cannot take place and you may start to experience the results of sleep deprivation, such as mood changes, low sex drive, poor balance, risk of heart disease, risk for diabetes, weight gain, high blood pressure, weakened immune system, mood changes, memory issues and loss of concentration. Sleep is just as important as any of the other pillars of wellness discussed in the book. As I said, it's probably the most overlooked. Having a balanced life that is vibrant and optimal takes more than eating right and going to the gym. Hence the house visual—we need all areas in balance or else our house will crumble.

I'm sure you have experienced what it's like to get really good restorative sleep and wake up feeling refreshed and full of energy. On those days, you're more productive, have an amazing workout, and are more laser-focused on your day-to-day activities. I've worked with so many people suffering from sleep deprivation who are trying to fuel their bodies with caffeine and sugar. It's a mess, and your whole body suffers. Then there are people who think it's completely normal to get up several times throughout the night. Yes, as we get older, we tend to take more trips to the bathroom at night, but a simple solution would be to cut off liquids before bed. We'll talk more about that in a bit.

Over the years, as I've worked with many clients on this sleep pillar, the same patterns and nightly routine habits causing their sleep issues frequently come up. Again, this list isn't exhaustive, but it's the top contenders:

- TV watching, computer use, phone use within two hours of bedtime
- Sleeping with the TV on
- Checking their phone or computer if they wake up
- Eating within two to three hours of bedtime
- Keeping their phone next to their bed with Wi-Fi on
- Sleeping in close proximity to a Wi-Fi router
- Wearing a sleep watch that emits EMFs (electromagnetic frequencies)
- Alcohol within six hours of bed
- Caffeine within twelve hours of bed
- Sleeping with a pet in their bed
- Having a partner in bed that snores

I'll go through these and explain why they negatively affect sleep and provide some simple solutions.

TV, COMPUTERS, PHONES

All these wonderful devices that we have grown to depend on daily can harm us in the evening hours due to the blue light they emit. What exactly is blue light? Blue light is very short high-energy waves, slightly less powerful than UV waves. How does blue light affect sleep? While the jury is still out on the long-term effects of blue light on human eye health, there is more consensus around the effects blue light has on your sleep-wake cycle. Light sensors in your eyes and even in your skin can perceive the difference between the intense blue light waves of bright daylight and the warmer, redder tones that signal the day is ending. When the light around you eases into those sunset shades, the sensors in your eyes prompt your body to release your body's natural stores of melatonin, the sleep-inducing hormone. A study conducted in 2015 found that people with greater blue light exposure in the evening experience significantly greater delays and disruption in their sleep cycles because it inhibits melatonin production.[13] A 2019 review found that blue light disturbances carry additional complications:

- Greater risk of hormone-induced cancers, including breast and prostate
- Diminished leptin levels, a chemical that signals food satiation to your body
- A number of metabolic changes, particularly blood sugar[14]

---

13 Anne-Marie Chang et al., "Evening use of light-emitting eReaders negatively affects sleep, circadian timing, and next-morning alertness," *PNAS* 112, no. 4 (December 22, 2014): 1232–1237, https://doi.org/10.1073/pnas.1418490112.
14 Christine Blume et al., "Effects of light on human circadian rhythms, sleep and mood," *Somnologie (Berl)* 23, no. 3 (August 20, 2019): 147–156, https://doi.org/10.1007/s11818-019-00215-x.

I remember a client I had several years back who continually fell asleep with the TV on. He was exhausted but loved watching late night sports. A game would end anywhere between 11:30 p.m. and 12 a.m., and he would fall asleep on the couch or chair until he woke up in the middle of the night. He would move to his bed, only to lay there unable to fall back asleep. His alarm went off at 6 a.m., so was averaging around two hours of sleep—and not even quality sleep! I know it's tough, guys, but taping a game or show and watching it the next day is always worth getting sleep. Especially when you are doing it on a consistent basis.

People tend to think they can "catch up" on sleep over the weekend, but in reality, that never happens because we have set a pattern with our sleep cycle. This is where discipline comes in. My husband went through a time when he kept waking up thinking about work. His mind just couldn't shut down. Instead of picking up his phone or computer, he would leave a notepad by the bed, write down the thought, and fall back asleep. We don't even sleep with phones in the bedroom anymore or have a TV in our room. We keep our room as dark as possible, and I suggest a sleep mask if it doesn't bother you. If you have to have your phone where you are sleeping, turn the Wi-Fi off or, better yet, put it in airplane mode. That way, the signals aren't waving through your room all night. For the same reasons, sleeping as far away from the Wi-Fi router is very important too. I know the watches that track sleep are so popular right now, but honestly, it's just another form of EMFs on your body while you sleep. I've had clients remove them and find an improvement in their sleep quality.

> **READING COMFORTING SCRIPTURES AND MEDITATING ON GOD'S WORD WAS A GAME CHANGER FOR ME.**

People often fall asleep with their TV on because it seems to curb loneliness, especially if they live alone. I remember when I was single and my kids went to their father's house for the weekend, I would get into a bad habit of sleeping on the couch with the TV on so that I didn't feel alone in the house. Thankfully, I realized that it wasn't doing me any good and disciplined myself to create a healthy nighttime routine. Reading comforting scriptures and meditating on God's Word was a game changer for me. I never felt alone and could fall asleep peacefully and stay asleep.

Something that I have recommended people try is falling asleep to light acoustic music or actual sleep music that has similar frequencies as the stages of sleep. I have tried that myself and really enjoy it. Another great idea is to fall asleep to scripture reading. There are apps you can download that play continual scripture. Remember, your body sleeps, but your spirit does not. You can nourish your spirit while your body rests.

Maybe you are doing all the right things and still having issues. I worked with another lady who would watch TV or a movie with her husband every night, right up to bedtime, while enjoying their favorite dish of ice cream or some other snack. She told me she was waking up every two hours after going to bed and couldn't stay asleep or get that deep sleep. I appreciate the fact they wanted to spend time doing something together, so I suggested that they play a card game, board game, or read together within one to two hours of bedtime. Also, the snacking had to stop. Every time we put food into our bodies, it will signal a response to use it for fuel. Your body will have to wake up and start processing the food. You don't need fuel or energy when you are winding down and getting ready for bed—which leads me to the next category of food and sleep.

CAFFEINE, ALCOHOL, AND FOOD
Caffeine

If I had a nickel for every time someone told me that caffeine doesn't affect their sleep, I'd be really wealthy. I get it—I'm Italian—and wine and espresso during and after dinner is a widely accepted thing. However, we need to make some choices that don't sacrifice our sleep. One gentleman told me that espresso after dinner doesn't hinder his sleep. Meanwhile, he's up every three hours using the bathroom during the night. Hmm... really? Consuming caffeine, which is a known stimulant, can greatly affect sleep within twelve hours of sleeping. In other words, if you go to bed at 9 p.m., it's a good idea to have your coffee first thing in the morning. IF you need to have that little kick in the afternoon, chances are your B vitamins are low, and a simple supplement could very well do the trick. If you *must* sip on something, I often recommend folks switch over to green tea. It has significantly less caffeine than coffee or black tea and is packed with antioxidants.

Alcohol

So many people enjoy a nightcap, but again, if I had a nickel for every time someone said, "Wine and liquor make me sleepy," I'd be a wealthy woman, and that's just it—they make you sleepy, but you don't stay asleep or get sound sleep because alcohol suppresses REM sleep. It's a relaxant and will help you fall asleep faster, but you will experience only light sleep and suffer sleep disturbances.

You may want to ask yourself why you need a substance to relax in the first place. If you are experiencing anxiety, racing thoughts, or stress, you may want to go back to the exercises on stress in the last chapter. We need REM sleep for brain development (which also helps combat racing thoughts and anxiety). Daily alcohol consumption may lead to full-blown insomnia because bodies develop a tolerance to the alcohol. The sugars in wine are another problem. Just like when you give a little kid too much candy and they get wound up, wine can do the same while it's relaxing you. It's like you have your foot on the gas and brake pedals at the same time.

If you do need a "nightcap," I suggest a nice cup of chamomile tea, tart cherry juice, or lemon balm tea. As I mentioned a minute ago, consuming any liquids before bed should be done within one to two hours before bedtime to reduce or eliminate middle-of-the-night bathroom trips.

Food

Eating late at night is never a good idea, especially if you're an early-to-bed/early riser like I am. I get to bed around 9 p.m. and get up at 5 a.m. every day, so eating dinner past 6 p.m. is pushing it if I want a good night's sleep. Eating right before bed or within two to three hours doesn't give your body a chance to digest your food. Remember food is fuel; it signals the body to turn on so it can be used. Most people don't need fuel to do anything when they wind down at night per se. Rather, food consumption is just for nourishment and replenishment of what's been used throughout our day.

> **OUR BRAIN, ORGANS, AND ENTIRE DIGESTIVE SYSTEM NEED A BREAK.**

I often tell my clients to think of their bodies as a factory that shuts down and sends everyone home at 5 p.m., not to return until the next morning. Every time we eat food past dinner time and close to bedtime, we open the doors to the factory, turn on the lights, and put the people back to work when they should be home resting and sleeping. Our brain, organs, and entire digestive system need a break. They work hard all day to keep us going, and we need to take good care of them by shutting down and letting them rest. Now, I'm not totally heartless. I understand there are occasions in life that come up, and we can't be so rigid all the time. I coach my clients on the 90/10 principle. If they are taking good care of their bodies 90 percent of the time (eating right, sleeping well, etc.) then the other 10 percent is manageable (weddings, parties, vacations). Even then, we don't need to go off the rails, but a late night here and there shouldn't be that problematic unless it becomes a regular habit. We can use food to set us up for a good night of sleep.

Getting adequate fiber is worth mentioning. A US survey of adults found that fiber intake predicted more time spent in the deep sleep state. Participants who reported adequate amounts of sleep (seven to nine hours) consumed the highest amounts of fiber. Complex carbohydrates (which are typically high in fiber) were also good for sleep.[15] The best fiber is found in whole plants (legumes, seeds, spinach, rice, sweet potatoes, oats, asparagus, and kale). These are great options to consume in the evening for dinner. They keep you fuller longer, curbing cravings and snacking.

Foods rich in magnesium are also great to eat before bed. Almonds, avocados, beetroot, quinoa, bananas, oats, spinach, and kidney beans are all great sources of magnesium. You can also try using a magnesium supplement or soaking in an Epsom salt bath to promote a state of relaxation. Tryptophan is the precursor to serotonin and is an essential amino acid to facilitate sleep. It can be found in turkey, kiwi, and almonds, to name a few. Many foods like mushrooms, honey, and oats contain melatonin, which is key for sleep. Do a little research of your own to see which foods you prefer and how you can incorporate them into your meals.

SLEEPING WITH PETS AND OTHER PEOPLE

If you share your bed with another person who keeps you awake with their snoring, movement, or other disturbances, my obvious suggestion is one of two things: invest in a pair of earplugs or sleep in another room if possible. I know that's not a popular option, but sleep is crucial to our overall health and well-being. If you are married, you can always make time for intimacy but then part ways to get quality sleep so that you are both refreshed and at your best for one another. Sometimes, it is the best thing you can do for

---

[15] Marie-Pierre St-Onge et al., "Fiber and Saturated Fat Are Associated with Sleep Arousals and Slow Wave Sleep," *Journal of Clinical Sleep Medicine* 12, no. 1 (January 15, 2016): 19–24, https://doi.org/10.5664/jcsm.5384.

your marriage. I have a client who has a very active sex life with her husband of thirty-nine years but they haven't *slept in* the same bed for years. She knows how important it is to get quality sleep, and they have an excellent relationship. As far as pets go, I know many people love them in their beds, but if they are disrupting your sleep, then that's a problem. You're not cruel or mean to have them sleep outside your room. If you have little people who find their way into your bed at night, that is a very personal choice, but again, be sure to prioritize sleep, so you can give them your best (not a cranky mommy or daddy who has been kept awake all night).

I hope you can see that prioritizing sleep is just as important as other areas of health and having a balanced life. A nightly routine is just as important as your morning routine. Just like you prepare for the day, you need to prepare for the evening and set yourself up for good quality sleep. Keep your room as dark as possible, use a sound machine if you need some background white noise, and be sure your area is comfy and inviting. We can't take it too lightly or take it for granted. Make small changes, a little at a time, if you're not ready to jump in and make a lot of changes at once. Pick one thing, try it for a week, and see how it goes. Those small changes will turn into daily habits that become new disciplines.

> *"Be sober [well balanced and self-disciplined], be alert and cautious at all times."*
> —1 Peter 5:8 (AMP)

PILLAR 5

FITNESS

The last wall of our "house" is going up! If you've ever built a new home, you know how exciting it is to have the frame finished and then have the roof put on. Our next two chapters make up the roof but this chapter is a real fan favorite... fitness! Fitness is a love-it-or-hate-it topic. Fitness means many different things to different people. For some, fitness could be a walk on their lunch break or after dinner. For others, fitness may mean hitting the gym multiple days a week to lift weights or take classes. For yet others, fitness is competition, such as a sport.

Recall the Bible verse I cited way back in chapter 1: "For physical training is of some value, but godliness has value for all things, holding promise for both the present life and the life to come" (1 Timothy 4:8, NIV). So, what does this have to do with fitness? If fitness is of little value, why bother? This scripture may appear to give folks an easy out. But I don't believe that is what God is telling us. Third John 1:2 tells us "Beloved, I pray that all may go well with you and that you may be in good health, as it goes well with your soul." God tells us that He wants us to be in good health. I think we can all agree that some type of fitness and movement will create good health in the body. A sedentary lifestyle will combat that.

One of many studies have found that a sedentary life is worse than smoking.[16] Being sedentary can set us up for all types of diseases and metabolic syndromes. Pay special attention to what God says in that verse: "as it goes well with your soul." That's our mind, will, and emotions. I see a direct correlation between good health in your body and your soul. Being active with some type of daily movement is very important to obtaining good health (and a balanced life) as is nourishing your spirit, eating well, managing stress, and sleeping well. By now, you can see that all these areas are necessary for building a quality home that will stand strong and endure. These areas need addressing to begin the balancing process in life.

I've been very disciplined with fitness my entire adult life. It is something I am passionate about. I was a certified personal trainer for many years and loved the gym atmosphere. There's something about the energy in a gym that is contagious. I was always very comfortable there and it became a second home. It is always incredible to see how the human body can transform when you exercise it. In addition to physical transformation, being active has many health benefits. The CDC website says the following:

> *Regular physical activity is one of the most important things you can do for your health. Being physically active can improve your brain health, help manage weight, reduce the risk of disease, strengthen bones and muscles, and improve your ability to do everyday activities.*[17]

---

16   Kyle Mandsager et al., "Association of Cardiorespiratory Fitness With Long-term Mortality Among Adults Undergoing Exercise Treadmill Testing," *JAMA Network Open* 1, no. 6 (October 19, 2018): e183605, https://doi.org/10.1001/jamanetworkopen.2018.3605.
17   "Benefits of Physical Activity," Physical Activity, Centers for Disease Control and Prevention, last reviewed August 1, 2023, https://www.cdc.gov/physicalactivity/basics/pa-health/index.htm#:~:text=Regular%20physical%20activity%20is%20one,ability%20to%20do%20everyday%20activities.

Who doesn't want all that, right? Adults who sit less and do any amount of moderate-to-vigorous physical activity will see health benefits. Only a few lifestyle choices have as large an impact on your health as physical activity. Everyone can experience the health benefits of physical activity no matter your age, ability, ethnicity, shape, or size. When I work with people who don't like the gym setting, I ask them what type of activity they *do* enjoy. It could be things like yard work, cycling, walking, swimming, etc. When they figure it out, I just tell them to keep doing it and do it more often and for longer periods of time. For example, if you enjoy a casual walk at lunch, add in another walk after dinner. Maybe you can increase your walk gradually over time. Start small and add on. If you only have time for a twenty-minute walk or bike ride, try to add on time and fit it into your schedule. Just be sure to incorporate something that moves your body consistently. Just like the other pillars, there's no way to sidestep fitness and achieve optimal health. Let's unpack the great benefits of being fit and incorporating everyday movement into our routine.

> **JUST LIKE THE OTHER PILLARS, THERE'S NO WAY TO SIDESTEP FITNESS AND ACHIEVE OPTIMAL HEALTH.**

THE BENEFITS OF PHYSICAL ACTIVITY

I would assume we all know that physical activity is good for us and provides many health benefits, but a lot of times, due to the demands and pressures of life, we often make excuses and somehow think we can make it up later or compensate in other areas. Exercise can sometimes feel like one more thing you have to add to your day, and I get it; I'm just like you, with a busy schedule and people who need me. Anytime we start a new habit or discipline, we need to have some patience with ourselves. Give yourself some grace as you add this to your daily routine. Here are just a few of the health benefits of being active. You may see that the very things that could hold us back, like being tired from poor sleep, are the very things that physical activity can help alleviate.

Weight Management

Both eating patterns and physical activity routines play a critical role in weight management. You gain weight when you consume more calories through eating and drinking than the number of calories you burn through physical activity.

Maintaining Your Weight

Work your way up to 150 minutes a week of moderate physical activity, which could include dancing or yard work. Pick anything that suits you. Shoot for 150 minutes a week—that's only thirty minutes a day, five days a week!

People vary greatly in how much physical activity they need for weight management. You may need more activity than others to reach or maintain a healthy weight. Seasons of life and certain health conditions are also factors. For example, if you are experiencing low hormones or an imbalance, doing a long HIIT exercise or heavy activity won't help you during that time. The body will require activity that is gentler and restorative, and the same applies when you are under heavy distress. Your body will do better with a gentler approach that doesn't take a lot out of it and raises the cortisol levels during that time.

To lose weight and keep it off, you will need a high amount of physical activity unless you also adjust your eating patterns and reduce the number of calories you're eating and drinking. Getting to and staying at a healthy weight requires both regular physical activity and healthy eating. However, losing weight will most often come from your diet, and then physical activity aids in that. First fuel the body, then it will perform well.

Echoing the same comment I made about adjusting your rigorous activity as the seasons of your life shift, your body is ever-changing. What worked at one time in your life may not work at another time. For most, menopause and midlife can be very challenging, and you may need to take those major life transitions into consideration. I certainly experienced this. I was in great stress and out of nowhere, my body started gaining some weight. My cortisol levels were high, and my hormones had completely tanked. When you work out like I do, heavy lifting and cardio were depleting all the energy reserves I had left. Even if you don't want to, it's very important to "listen" to your body and not push it. I had to cut back for a bit until my body settled and came back into balance.

Reduces Health Risks

Exercising regularly can prevent many sicknesses and diseases.

1) Cardiovascular Disease

Heart disease and stroke are two leading causes of death in the United States. Getting at least 150 minutes a week of moderate physical activity can put you at a lower risk for these diseases. You can reduce your risk even further with more physical activity. Regular physical activity can also lower your blood pressure and improve your cholesterol levels.

2) Type 2 Diabetes and Metabolic Syndrome

Regular physical activity can reduce your risk of developing type 2 diabetes and metabolic syndrome. Metabolic syndrome is a combination of too much fat around the waist, high blood pressure, low high-density lipoproteins (HDL) cholesterol, high triglycerides, or high blood sugar. Even people who *don't* meet the recommended 150 minutes a week of moderate physical activity may start to see benefits, but additional amounts of physical activity seem to lower risk even more.

3) Infectious Diseases

Physical activity may help reduce the risk of serious infectious diseases, including colds, flu, and pneumonia. For example:

- People who are minimally physically active are more likely to contract and experience the most extreme cold than those who regularly engage in physical activity. A systematic CDC review discovered that higher levels of physical activity were linked to fewer hospitalizations and deaths. The risk increased significantly for inactive participants.[18]
- Flu or pneumonia may be less fatal the more active you are. A CDC study found that adults who meet the physical activity criteria for aerobic and muscle-strengthening guidelines

---

18   Aisha L. Hill et al., review of *Brief Summary of Findings on the Association Between Physical Inactivity and Severe COVID-19 Outcomes*, reviewed by Aisha L. Hill et al., Centers for Disease Control and Prevention, 1-63, https://www.cdc.gov/coronavirus/2019-ncov/downloads/Brief-Summary-of-Findings-on-the-Association-Between-Physical-Inactivity-and-Severe-COVID-19-Outcomes.pdf.

are 50 percent less likely to die from flu and pneumonia compared to adults who did not meet the criteria for either.[19]

4) Some Cancers

Being physically active lowers your risk for developing several common cancers. Adults who participate in greater amounts of physical activity have reduced risks of developing cancers of the following:
- Bladder
- Breast
- Colon (proximal and distal)
- Endometrium
- Esophagus (adenocarcinoma)
- Kidney
- Lung
- Stomach (cardia and non-cardia adenocarcinoma)

If you are a cancer survivor, getting regular physical activity not only helps give you a better quality of life but also improves your physical fitness.

Strengthen Your Bones and Muscles

As you age, it's important to protect your bones, joints, and muscles; they support your body and help you move. Keeping bones, joints, and muscles healthy can help ensure that you're able to do your daily activities and remain physically active.

Muscle-strengthening activities like lifting weights can help you increase or maintain your muscle mass and strength. This is important for older adults who experience reduced muscle

---

[19] Bryant J. Webber et al., "Leisure-time physical activity and mortality from influenza and pneumonia: a cohort study of 577,909 US adults," *British Journal of Sports Medicine* 57, no. 19 (2023): 1231–1237, https://doi.org/10.1136/bjsports-2022-106644.

mass and muscle strength with aging. Slowly increasing the amount of weight and number of repetitions you do as part of muscle-strengthening activities will bring even greater benefits, no matter your age.

Improve Your Ability to Do Daily Activities and Prevent Falls

Everyday activities include climbing stairs, grocery shopping, or playing with your kids and grandkids. Being unable to do everyday activities is called a functional limitation. Physically active middle-aged or older adults have a lower risk of functional limitations than inactive people.

For older adults, doing a variety of physical activities improves physical function and decreases the risk of falls or injury from a fall. Include physical activities such as aerobics, muscle strengthening, and balance training in your exercise protocol. Multicomponent physical activity can be done at home or in a community setting as part of a structured program. Perimenopause can start as early as the late 30s for some women. When I went through that, I noticed my balance was off. Some of the exercises I had grown accustomed to became a bit more challenging due to wonky hormones, and it was more difficult to keep my balance. So, I had to adjust. I incorporated a balance board or Bosu ball when I was at the gym. I've learned to never take my balance for granted.

Hip fracture is a serious health condition that can result from a fall. Breaking a hip has life-changing negative effects, especially if you're an older adult. Physically active people have a lower risk of hip fracture than inactive people. Even if you are younger and active, a hip fracture or hip issue is debilitating.

I know plenty of younger adults who have already had hip surgery and or replacements.

Increase Your Chances of Living Longer

Taking more steps daily also helps lower the risk of premature death from all causes. For adults younger than sixty, the risk of premature death leveled off at about 8,000 to 10,000 steps per day. For adults sixty and older, the risk of premature death leveled off at about 6,000 to 8,000 steps per day.

Manage Chronic Health Conditions and Disabilities

Regular physical activity can help people manage existing chronic conditions and disabilities. For example, regular physical activity can:

- Reduce pain and improve function, mood, and quality of life for adults with arthritis. I can't emphasize enough how much physical activity impacts your mood. So many people struggle with depression and anxiety, but when you are active, your brain produces good chemicals such as serotonin, dopamine, and endorphins. These are the "feel good" chemicals. In addition, it's a great stress reliever.
- Help control blood sugar levels and lower the risk of heart disease and nerve damage for people with type 2 diabetes. I've worked with people who successfully reverse type 2 with just diet and exercise.
- Help support daily living activities and independence for people with disabilities. Physical disabilities can be permanent or temporary. Either way, a fitness program can be tailored to work for any circumstance. For example, I have

continued my workouts while sustaining an injury. Also, I know several people in a wheelchair who work out and have tremendous upper body strength. Those people take the "no excuses" approach, and I love it!

Just like anything, being fit is a choice. It must become a discipline that you incorporate into your daily life, just like brushing your teeth or any other daily habit. Fitness is an essential part of a balanced wellness regimen. If you don't like lifting weights or going to a gym, which is a common complaint I hear from older people and some women, I ask them to challenge themselves by carefully lifting heavier objects throughout their day (a gallon of laundry detergent or other weighty object). Our muscles atrophy very quickly, and those muscles protect our skeletal system. It's so important to give every part of our body attention, so it will continue to maintain and carry us through our lives.

If you are a relatively healthy younger or average-aged person, I encourage you to incorporate strength training in addition to cardio workouts. Remember that you can get a great workout if you are doing it efficiently. People don't need to spend hours at the gym doing any form of fitness routine if it is done properly, and you can maximize your time for great results. Also, ladies, don't be afraid of the weights. So many women think that weights will make them look "bulky," and my response has always been, "Weights make you strong, cupcakes make you look bulky." When you go to a fitness center, you see mostly women on the treadmills and bikes. The average number of women in the free weight area is twenty-seven men to one woman. We need to change that, ladies. My seventy-seven-year-old neighbor goes to the gym every morning, and bless her heart, she is in there lifting weights with the guys and loving every minute of it. I always tell her that I want to be her when I grow up!

Physical training is the only non-pharmaceutical intervention that, when done consistently, will offset age-related declines in strength. In addition to keeping us strong, it is also the best non-pharmaceutical known to improve mood. The Bible speaks of staying strong in Hebrews 12:12: "Therefore lift your drooping hands and strengthen your weak knees."

So many challenges in life can try to take us out and get us down. Staying strong in our spirit is our number one priority and keeps us grounded and encouraged with hope. Being well in our soul—what we think and feel—is also important. The soul is closely tied to our spirit, but then our bodies should also be aligned (balanced) with strength to finish this life strong. If you are a Christian, a follower of Jesus Christ, then you know we have a big job here, and that is to represent Jesus. We are His ambassadors. He certainly wasn't a weakling. No, sir. Don't ever mistake His kind and gentle heart for physical or emotional weakness. He is our strong tower. The Bible says in Proverbs 18:10 (NKJV), "The name of the LORD *is* a strong tower; The righteous run to it and are safe." It took incredible physical and emotional strength for Him to go to the cross for us, and the same incredible love and strength held Him there.

Increases Your Quality of Sleep

John Hopkins Medical stated that those who exercise regularly experience higher-quality sleep.[20] People who engage in at least

---

20 "Sleeping well at night makes every day better," *John Hopkins University*, 16 March 2023, https://hub.jhu.edu/at-work/2023/03/16/sleeping-well/#:~:text=You%20might%20be%20less%20sleepy,least%20three%20hours%20before%20bedtime.

thirty minutes of moderate aerobic exercise may see a difference in sleep quality that same night. It generally will not take months or years to see results. Moderate aerobic exercise increases the amount of slow-wave sleep you get. Slow-wave sleep is your deep sleep, where the brain and body have a chance to rejuvenate. Exercise can also help stabilize your mood and decompress your mind.

GETTING STARTED WITH A FITNESS REGIMEN

If you would categorize yourself as someone who is not engaging in regular fitness but wants to get started, here are a few simple tips that will work for any age:

1) Start small. Don't set out to run a marathon if you haven't run before. There are so many wonderful fitness apps available today to help people get started. The same goes for strength training or any other type of class such as swimming, cycling, or Pilates. Find a good instructor, class, or trainer that can guide you as well as motivate and encourage you. Start with two or three days per week and then add on.

2) Find an activity that you enjoy. It's safe to say that most of us won't continue anything fitness-related if we aren't enjoying it. Biking, walking, running, swimming, and strength training are all wonderful options, but may not be right for every person. Be sure it is something you can do consistently. It is always a great idea to find a friend to work out with.

3) Make it a lifestyle habit. Just like any other habit you do daily, fitness should be included. However, our bodies need days to rest and recover. Walking can be done daily, but you need recovery days for strength training or heavy resistance-type

exercises. More isn't always better when it comes to fitness. Results happen on recovery and rest days.

THINGS TO CONSIDER WHEN YOU'VE PLATEAUED

1) With age comes wisdom ... and also some unwanted visitors such as hormonal changes and extra pressures.

Hormone imbalance is very common as we approach middle age. It is also becoming alarmingly common among the younger generation due to the added hormones in animal products that we consume. Endocrine disruptors are found in our makeup, personal care items, and household cleaners as well as the "fragrance" candles and deodorizers, to name a few. Being vigilant to inspect ingredient labels will help you tremendously.

I worked with a gentleman who was going through andropause. I'd see him often at the gym, and one day he said he wanted to start working with me because he knew something was off. He wasn't seeing results from the hard work he was putting in and needed some help figuring it out. By changing out some household products and personal care items, as well as cleaning up his diet, he noticed a marked improvement in energy. Men and women can also balance hormones with the proper nutrition. There are times when it is necessary to get labs to see what your hormones are doing. It's very common in mid-life for women to experience drops in estrogen (and other hormones) which will contribute to unexplained weight gain ... which is what happened to me. I suggest that if it persists, you find a qualified doctor who specializes in hormones to help you.

> **THERE ARE TIMES TO PUSH THROUGH AND TIMES TO REST, BUT KNOWING YOUR BODY IS KEY.**

Stress will also lead to mood imbalance, energy depletion, and overall feelings of no motivation. It's perfectly normal to go through those seasons in life. As mentioned in the stress chapter, there are ways to help mitigate it for optimal results from your workouts. Depending on the cause, a good workout will be beneficial, even if you don't feel up to it. There are times to push through and times to rest, but knowing your body is key. Don't push through if you are physically unwell; that will only exacerbate the problem.

2) Proper nutrition is critical when we work out and try to reach our goals.

If you feel you have hit a plateau, you may need to adjust your macronutrients. One of the biggest challenges people face is getting adequate amounts of protein each day. That looks different for everyone depending on your age, the type of workouts you do, and the goals you have set for yourself. I suggest working with a nutrition specialist or a health care provider to be sure you are getting the adequate amounts of macronutrients specific to your needs.

3) Different seasons of life may require us to change it up a bit.

I've worked with a lot of women, and most have incorporated fitness into their daily routine for years. What I have found is that rigorous workouts don't always serve us well in the middle of a big life event or menopause. Backing off can be a hard concept to embrace. Most fitness enthusiasts tend to have a fear of losing all their gains or regression. Getting your body back into balance should be your number one priority. *Then* build a fitness routine that works to support it.

IT'S WORTH IT, AND YOU CAN DO IT

We should all strive toward being fit for many reasons. Besides making our bodies strong, a routine fitness regimen strengthens our immune system and makes us resilient to sickness. It improves mood. (Let's be honest, we all feel better when we participate in some type of physical activity.) As a note of encouragement, just start small if exercise is new for you or doesn't come easily. Two to three days per week of thirty minutes of movement can greatly impact your health. If you want to incorporate new things into your fitness routine, seek out a friend to join you or hire a personal trainer who can guide and encourage you on your journey. Being fit shouldn't feel like a "chore" but a blessing to keep our bodies well-maintained to live our lives to the fullest and be healthy and well for the ones we love and care about the most.

PILLAR 6

RELATIONSHIPS

Our "house" is starting to look more like a "home" as we build the roof with these final two chapters. In this chapter, we will talk about relationships and why they are so vitally important for us. We all have them, and as long as we are here on earth and even into eternity, we will have relationships. In the Bible, Genesis 2:18 says, "Then the LORD God said, 'It is not good that man should be alone; I will make him a helper fit for him.'" When I read that, several things come to mind. First, before God made the helper for Adam, Adam and God had a relationship (see Genesis 2:7 where God formed him from the dust). However, God made Adam in His image, as a human man, so God knew it wouldn't be good for him to be alone. But wait a minute, if Adam already had God, and Genesis 1:25–27 says that God created the animals that were with Adam always, why did God still consider Adam alone? It's not that God wasn't enough for Adam. He just designed Adam to have relationships with other humans.

Another mystery of God.

That's how He designed us. God made Adam a suitable helpmate, a woman. God then lays out His intention for them in Genesis 1:28 (KJV):

> *And God blessed them, and God said unto them, "Be fruitful, and multiply, and replenish the earth, and subdue it: and have dominion over the fish of the sea, and over the fowl of the air, and over every living thing that moveth upon the earth."*

> **GOD COULD HAVE POPULATED THE EARTH HIMSELF, BUT HE DIDN'T. HE TASKED THE MAN AND WOMAN TO DO THAT.**

Another thought to ponder: God could have populated the earth Himself, but He didn't. He tasked the man and woman to do that. I find that so fascinating. God wants us to enjoy relationships. They should be healthy and nourishing to us. As in the first marriage relationship, we see that it was to be fruitful. Another verse that I love is found in Ecclesiastes 4:10 and 12:

> *For if they fall, one will lift up his fellow. But woe to him who is alone when he falls and has not another to lift him up. . . . And though a man might prevail against one who is alone, two will withstand him—a threefold cord is not quickly broken.*

We are stronger when we are with others. Proverbs 27:17 proclaims that "iron sharpens iron, and one man sharpens another." We are better together, stronger, and sharper when we have the right people around us.

I've come across many folks who say they like animals more than people. While it's awesome to love our pets (I sure do) when I hear that, I think it's because someone has hurt them in the past and typically, our pets don't hurt us. They give us unconditional love, which is at the heart of every person—to be fully loved and accepted. But if God wanted that for Adam, He would have left him alone with all his animals and never made Eve. I think it's very important to understand that a lot of times, we don't expect others to let us down and hurt us, but they will—either intentionally or unintentionally. We all can think of a time we hurt someone close to us unintentionally. We are imperfect human beings. Only God is perfect, and He is the only One capable of perfect love without hurt. Though our relationship with Him should be our number one priority, He created us to love one another. In Matthew 22:36–39 (NIV), Jesus's disciples asked Him about the greatest commandments:

"Teacher, which is the greatest commandment in the law?" Jesus replied, "'Love the Lord your God with all your heart and with all your soul and with all your mind.' This is the first and greatest commandment. And the second is like it: 'Love your neighbor as yourself.'"

Relationships can bring us great joy and happiness, but some can bring us enormous stress and sorrow. When I coach my clients through this pillar of the balanced life method, I have them examine the relationships in their lives. We focus on both the happy and the sad. In fact, I am coaching a client right now on relationships. She has a stressful family situation with a very troubled adult child. Her daughter-in-law is a narcissist and causes much strife and contention in the family. She has been carrying this around, and it's affecting her well-being dramatically. This is obviously a tough situation, especially since she only has very limited visitation privileges with her grandson. My heart breaks for her.

When we first started working together four months ago, her voice and hands would visibly shake when she spoke about her situation—you could see how much the topic hurt her. She was letting this control her joy and happiness. I didn't suggest she pretend as if everything was okay. Instead, we worked through some forgiveness issues and new thought processes she could implement. As a result, she started to view this woman as a hurting person who suffered trauma as a child and is now acting out her wounds. We can't control other people; we can only control our reactions. Since this is a close family member that she can't just dismiss from her life, she needed to take control of her reactions so that she didn't get sick from them. She is a believer in Jesus and knows the power of His name. When the devil would torment her thoughts (especially in the middle of the night, waking her up) she didn't know what to do. But now, she rebukes the enemy (the devil), chooses to cling to God's promises, and can fall back to sleep.

THE WAR ON RELATIONSHIPS

Ever since Adam and Eve were in the garden, there has been a war on relationships. Most of us know the account of the serpent (Satan, the devil) who deceived Eve into eating the apple from the forbidden tree, which she then gave to her husband Adam. When God approached Adam about the situation, his first reaction was to blame his wife, and then she proceeded to blame the serpent.

Do you see it? That's where it all began. Satan hates relationships and will cause division whenever and wherever he can. He is still doing it today, but most of us are unaware and just think it's normal to have these disputes with other people. I mean, honestly, we can't get along with everyone, right? We are commanded to *love* them but not necessarily be in relationship with them. I'll get to that in a little bit when we talk about setting boundaries.

For now, a basic awareness that God loves relationships and the enemy hates them gives us a good understanding when we process our own relationships. The enemy causes division, but God creates unity. Christian or not, you may be familiar with the verse in Ephesians 6:12 (KJV), "For we wrestle not against flesh and blood, but against principalities, against powers, against the rulers of the darkness of this world, against spiritual wickedness in high places." If you're not familiar, you may be wondering what exactly that means. It means that we don't fight with each other; we are fighting with a "dark spirit" that is either IN the person or strongly influencing them. As I mentioned in chapter 1, we know that the enemy will make a grand entrance into our lives when we let him in (even if it's unknowingly). Trauma is often his way in. We'll unpack this more later, but the enemy will infect our soul wounds (trauma) that will perpetuate in our relationships (like multiple failed marriages or jobs).

I am fully aware that there are just some people you cannot unite with, perhaps due to their own trauma and soul wounds. My client is a great example of this. It's difficult for her to be united and reconciled to her daughter-in-law because her daughter-in-law doesn't think there is a problem. She takes no ownership. You, too, may be experiencing that in a relationship. I know I have. It's extremely difficult, especially when it's a very close relationship. But it is our responsibility to control how we think, act, and talk about them. First Peter 4:8 (NIV) says, "Above all, love each other deeply because love covers over a multitude of sins." It is our job to protect our hearts also. We love from our hearts. Love is not just a feeling; it is an action and a choice. We have free will to choose to love others with our actions and words.

> **WE LOVE FROM OUR HEARTS. LOVE IS NOT JUST A FEELING; IT IS AN ACTION AND A CHOICE.**

Proverbs 4:23 (NIV) says, "Above all else, guard your heart, for everything you do flows from it." As I'm writing this, I'm asking the Holy Spirit for guidance because this is such an important part of our lives here on earth and one that I feel gets attacked the most. The enemy knows how important healthy, strong relationships are to us. He is outnumbered when we are in unity together. His destructive plans fail when we fight the real enemy together and not each other. Remember how Adam and Eve were deceived. The deception ultimately caused division, and the enemy weaved his works into their family for generations—you and I are no different. I've worked with so many people over the years, and in my own experiences, I see how hurt relationships can just shatter a person, whether the fissure happened in childhood with an adult or parent or later in life from someone very close. These leave soul wounds that, more often than not, never get healed because we are unaware of them.

Yet another form of warfare on relationships.

WHAT IS A SOUL WOUND?

Our soul is made up of the mind, will, and emotions (heart). All of us have been hurt or traumatized by something or someone in our lives. When the wound is never healed (which I personally believe that only Jesus Himself can do), it forms an alternate personality in us or traits that we weren't born with. Remember, God created us in His image. Any other traits or behaviors we exhibit apart from His perfect nature come from what we have experienced. Yes, we get certain traits and characteristics from our parents and others who raised us, but I'm always curious to know how much of who we become is genetic and how much of it comes from observing others when we were young and impressionable. Either way, when we are hurt, it wounds our soul. For example, when parents or caregivers make a child feel rejected or unloved, that child could develop avoidant tendencies in relationships as an adult because they are fearful of being hurt in a new intimate relationship. They can't trust. This avoidance is mostly unconscious.

As adults, a divorce, harsh words, a betrayal, or a rejection could wound us and leave scars. When that happens, walls are built as a means of protection. People can develop mistrusting tendencies and take them from relationship to relationship, leaving a wake of perpetual damage. These traumas also get passed down generationally. Notice how patterns repeat in families. Anger is a big one. A man or woman has anger issues, and so did his father, and so did his grandmother. Coincidence? I don't think so. While it could be a learned behavior, it could also be generational trauma that keeps getting passed down until someone seeks help to heal the soul wounds and put an end to their tyranny.

We need to put an end to hurtful patterns and tendencies that cause division, and healing them is the only way to stop them. Yes, we can work on behavior modification, but it's like putting a Band-Aid on a gaping wound—it only helps for a short time, but sooner or later, it needs to be addressed, so true healing can begin. There are many good resources on emotional healing. I went through this myself several years ago. I saw repeated patterns that I knew weren't right, and I wanted to address them so that I could experience life the way God intended before the trauma entered my world as a child. I needed healing from traumas and soul wounds that took place in my adult life too. The process isn't difficult; it just starts with recognizing and accepting they are there.

Take an inventory of situations or people that seem to "trigger" you or set off negative emotions. Think of an event that happened when you first felt that negative emotion. Think of how it made you feel and name the negative emotion. If it has caused sinful behavior in your life, then confession and repentance need to come first. After you ask God to forgive you for acting out in sin, ask Jesus to heal your soul. Tell him you don't want that negative emotion anymore, and ask Him to replace it with the right one. Keep repeating the process as many times as necessary until you are left with no feeling at all. When that soul wound finally heals, the toxic cycles stop. Maybe you keep picking the wrong friend group or find yourself attracted to the wrong person in romantic relationships. These cyclical patterns likely stem from a wound in need of healing. When the wound is healed, you can make healthy choices.

In my healing process, I was asked to think about situations that left me feeling unworthy, vulnerable, unprotected, and terrified. After each negative emotion came up, I asked Jesus to come in and heal that wound. After the healing, I felt loved and special instead of unworthy. I felt protected and safe instead of terrified and vulnerable. When I got to the end of all the negative emotions, I thought about that situation again, and not a single one of those feelings came up. I literally felt nothing negative, and still don't to this very day. My soul was healed, and I'm so thankful.

A lot of people miss this. We live in a culture that labels people. We label them depressed, anxious, angry, crazy, disassociated, bipolar, borderline, etc. I mean no disrespect to all the practicing psychologists out there, but I believe at the heart of almost everyone, some trauma needs addressing and healing. We can talk it out for years in therapy and stay on medication, which may be a good temporary measure, but only Jesus, who bore our grief and sorrows on the cross, along with our sin, can heal. Consider the scriptures in Isaiah 53:3–5 (NIV):

He was despised and rejected by mankind, a man of suffering, and familiar with pain. Like one from whom people hide their faces he was despised, and we held him in low esteem. Surely, he took up our pain and bore our suffering, yet we considered him punished by God, stricken by him, and afflicted. But he was pierced for our transgression, he was crushed for our iniquities, the punishment that brought us peace was on him, and by his wounds we are healed.

That is so powerful! In church, we often hear Jesus died for our sins, but we don't hear much about everything else He hung there for. He bore our sorrows (soul wounds), and that verse says that by his wounds we are healed. A lot of people just think that means physical healing from a sickness, but mental health issues and emotional issues are all part of it.

> **YOU MAY HAVE RECEIVED THE GIFT OF FORGIVENESS FOR YOUR SINS TO SECURE YOUR ETERNAL HOME, BUT HAVE YOU RECEIVED THE HEALING HE WANTS TO GIVE YOU THROUGH HEALING YOUR SOUL?**

Let me just shout, "Hallelujah!"

He loved us so much that He took it all. Receiving Jesus as your Lord and Savior is a personal choice just like receiving the healing. You may have received the gift of forgiveness for your sins to secure your eternal home, but have you received the healing He wants to give you through healing your soul? If not, and this is the first time you're hearing about this, I encourage you to spend some time learning more or personally reaching out to me.

FORGIVENESS, RESTORATION, AND RECONCILIATION

There is so much misconception when I work with folks on these topics. We'll go through them and define what they are and what they are not. I think you will be able to see how they impact relationships.

Forgiveness

We've all been hurt by other people's words or actions, which leaves *us* with a choice to forgive or not forgive. First, forgiveness is not a feeling. You may never "feel" forgiveness. Forgiveness is an act of will. It may sound something like, "I give up the right to hurt that person back." You may not intend to physically hurt them, but you can hurt them with passive-aggressive behavior, snarky comments, disrespect, and dishonor. If you choose to forgive, you leave their punishment up to God who says in Romans 12:19 (NIV), "Do not take revenge, my dear friends, but leave room for God's wrath, for it is written: 'It is mine to avenge; I will repay,' says the Lord." While forgiveness is our choice, God is very clear in His Word about it.

Matthew 6:14-15 (NLT) says: "If you forgive those who sin against you, your heavenly Father will forgive you. But, if you refuse to forgive others, your Father will not forgive your sins." Pretty direct and sobering, huh? It is tempting to hang on to the offenses of others. Remember our enemy, the devil, will always try to divide us, and he will whisper thoughts in our heads to keep us trapped in unforgiveness. I've heard it said that unforgiveness is like drinking poison and expecting the person who hurt you to die. Unforgiveness only hurts *us*. Most times, the offender doesn't even care or know how hurt you are. If however, they do know, and come to you and ask for forgiveness, it becomes your choice. People tend to think that forgiving is letting the other person off the hook and making light of the offense. But that's not true because God sees all, and He knows all. He will take care of the matter in His timing.

I've seen unforgiveness make people physically sick in their bodies. They refuse to forgive someone who hurt them years ago and keep drinking the poison. They won't let it go. It's sad. I've had to forgive some pretty awful things in my life with people who are very close to me, and I can tell you that there is no better feeling than to forgive and let it go and trust God with it. I no longer had to carry it. Maybe you're someone who can forgive others easily, but when it comes to yourself, you can't. This is something else that I had to learn. It seems everything I had to learn I am now able to help others walk through.

> **WHEN WE FORGIVE OURSELVES, IT BECOMES EASIER TO FORGIVE OTHERS.**

Forgiving ourselves is also critical to healing. When we accept that we are all sinful and flawed individuals with wounds from our past that create dysfunctional tendencies and thought processes, we see how hurtful it can be to keep carrying those mistakes from our past around. When we don't forgive ourselves, it not only affects us but others around us. For example, I worked with a woman who had made some very poor choices in her life. She had a husband and family who had no idea about what I would call her "secret life." On the outside, she seemed happy-go-lucky besides battling depression, weight issues, and other health challenges.

When we worked through the origin of her poor decisions, she discovered it was childhood trauma that distorted her thinking and drove her actions. She needed to forgive her parents, as well as herself. Thankfully, she stopped her risky behavior and was able to get off some of the psychoactive medications she was taking and really take hold of her health once and for all. She worked through forgiveness with her parents, and she was able to forgive herself. When we forgive ourselves, it becomes easier to forgive others.

One of my closest and longtime friends opened up after years of keeping a dark secret that she hadn't forgiven herself for. One day, she had a revelation from God; whether He spoke to her directly, I don't know, but she just felt in her spirit that if she continued to punish herself for the horrible choice she made when she was young, she was essentially telling God that what Jesus did on the cross wasn't enough. She was coming into agreement with the enemy's whispers: "Your sin is too big, too bad, and too much to forgive." It was then that she knew that the price Jesus paid on the cross covered ALL and every sin that every person had or will ever commit. Examine your own heart and start with yourself.

Maybe the person you need to forgive is . . . you.

Reconciliation

This can only happen when the offender repents and the offended forgives. So many relationships are broken due to unforgiveness and unrepentance. Without them, you can't have reconciliation. A person who never owns up to their actions will never experience reconciliation with the one they hurt. They may be forgiven, but not reconciled.

I just want to make a point here about reconciliation. There are times and situations where a relationship does not need to be reconciled. I am a case in point.

My grandmother's husband sexually abused me as a child. Both have since passed away. I told my family about the abuse. He was confronted and eventually apologized. I forgave him; however, that was one relationship that did not need to be reconciled or restored. No good would come of it. I left it in the past. Each situation should be handled with care and prayer to see what God would lead you to do. In my case, I felt very comfortable with my decision.

Restoration

This can only happen in a healthy way after reconciliation. Some hurts are very deep. Infidelity in a marriage is a classic example of profound pain that leaves behind scars of mistrust and severed intimacy. Restoring will take time—time to restore the relationship to where it once was. The same goes for a business relationship where a partner may have betrayed another. After the offender confesses and seeks forgiveness and the offended party grants forgiveness, they can then begin the process of restoring the relationship. In cases like these, restoration is the best way to go if both parties are willing to put in the work and take time to discover why the hurt or betrayal happened in the first place.

I want to mention how relationships can affect health more than we could ever know or understand. Even the relationship we have with ourselves can affect our health. The way we think about ourselves and treat ourselves is huge when it comes to our health. Let's say you made some poor decisions in your past that you can't forgive yourself for or let go of. You may have developed this mantra: "I'm such a loser"—maybe you don't say it out loud, but in your head and your heart, you feel nothing good should come to you because you are unworthy. Those are lies from the pit of hell. Possibly, you are in a very stressful marriage or other relationship that creates distress. This could lead to weight gain, depression, anxiety, and high blood pressure, just to name a few. Our natural tendency is to look for the cause on a genetic level, but in reality, what's going on around us is the most impactful on our well-being.

HEALTHY BOUNDARIES IN RELATIONSHIPS

Let's start with a simple definition of a boundary. In her book *Boundaries: Where You End and I Begin*, Anne Katherine states, "A boundary is a limit or edge that defines you as separate from others."[21]

Having boundaries is very important in relationships. It will keep the integrity of both parties intact. Let's suppose you are a people pleaser by nature, have a hard time saying no, and find yourself being taken advantage of at times. You would need to identify this and actually set a boundary so as not to overextend yourself and say yes to everything. Doing so enables others to continue taking from you. Setting boundaries will protect you from people running you down and running you over. I know people who are givers to the point of debilitating exhaustion. People will keep taking as long as you keep giving. At some point, there needs to be reciprocation if it is a healthy relationship. Setting

---
[21] Anne Katherine, *Boundaries: Where You end and I Begin* (New York, NY: Fireside, 1991) 14.

healthy boundaries also keeps us from developing bitterness and resentment toward others.

> **SETTING BOUNDARIES WILL PROTECT YOU FROM PEOPLE RUNNING YOU DOWN AND RUNNING YOU OVER.**

Our skin is an obvious physical boundary, but we have other kinds of interpersonal boundaries too, including a limit that extends beyond our body. Consider what happens when somebody stands too close for comfort. We often describe it as someone invading our personal space, but definitions of personal space vary according to culture, the type of relationship, and social context. The boundaries you set with your partner at home would be inappropriate in a different social context, such as a business dinner.

Boundaries differ from person to person and are mediated by variations in culture, personality, and social context. Appropriate boundaries in a business meeting would seem irrelevant in an outing with old friends. Setting boundaries defines our expectations of ourselves and others in different kinds of relationships. Similarly, the level of physical intimacy deemed appropriate for expression in public spaces varies wildly across cultures. For example, in Sri Lanka, it is customary for children to greet their parents by touching their feet rather than hugging them. Meanwhile, touching, hugging, and kissing between married couples is frowned upon in public. Here in the US, we typically greet other people we know with a hug, kiss, or handshake.

Setting healthy boundaries requires self-awareness. We need to be clear about our expectations of ourselves and others and what we are and are not comfortable with in specific situations. Setting healthy boundaries requires good communication skills that convey assertiveness and clarity.

Assertiveness involves expressing your feelings openly and respectfully. It does not entail making demands, but it requires that people listen to you as you assert your needs and priorities. Yes, boundary setting is a form of self-care! Here are three easy steps to setting boundaries in relationships:

Step 1. Be as clear and as straightforward as possible. Do not raise your voice.

Step 2. Directly state your need or request in terms of what you'd like rather than what you don't want or like.

Step 3. Accept any discomfort that arises as a result, whether it's guilt, shame, or remorse.

Note: Guilt, shame, and remorse are common for people with poor boundaries, codependency issues, and people pleasers. That being said, those individuals may find their "aha!" moment and discover the deeper issues that need addressing when they accept the discomfort. Only then will they be fully equipped to seek help.

Sometimes, adults have been raised by childhood caregivers who've taught them that expressing their needs is bad and selfish. However, not accepting the discomfort that comes from setting healthy boundaries in adulthood means settling for unhealthy relationships that can cause resentment, manipulation, and abuse.

When we are dealing with people who repeatedly cross or violate our personal boundaries, then the whole nature of the relationship may need to change. This can be tricky when we cannot escape that person, such as a coworker or family member. In such situations, you may have to communicate the consequences this way: "I've communicated with you as simply as I can, and if you cannot respect my needs as a person, I will have to _____ or _____ will have to happen." Be sure to state why this is important to you.

Understanding that you are valuable and worthy of being treated well in relationships is very important. Like I just mentioned, it starts with how we view ourselves. There's a saying: "People will only treat you on the basis of what you tolerate." Maybe you need to start with forgiving yourself before you are able to put your foot down when others mistreat you. These issues span across ALL relationships: spouses, in-laws, parents, children, your boss, your coworkers, and more. We are very valuable creations of God, and we should all be treated as such.

Who Are You Surrounding Yourself with?

You become who you hang around. I know this sounds trite, but you'd be surprised at how many people I work with know they shouldn't be associating with certain people in their life. People who bring you down, speak negatively all the time, or try to persuade you to think or do things you may not be inclined to do—all red flags. I hate to say it, but there are just some friends that we outgrow. If you are a married person, and your best friend is recently divorced and all they do is talk poorly about marriage and how awesome their newfound freedom is, what kind of effect do you think that will have on you? Pretty soon, you may start thinking thoughts you don't normally think. They may invite you to go out with them and mingle in places that you wouldn't normally go. On the other hand, surrounding yourself with other people who have strong marriages will also impact you . . . but for the better. Remember the old saying, "One bad apple spoils the whole bag"? What about 1 Corinthians 15:33 (NIV): "Do not be misled: 'Bad company corrupts good character'"?

When you take inventory of your relationships, consider these questions: Are they making me into who I want to be? Do they cause me distress or bring me down? Like I mentioned, you may find there are some you need to limit your time with or protect yourself from altogether.

Take boundaries seriously.

Living Life Unoffended Is the Goal, and Compassion Is the Only Way

The world seems to be full of easily offended people today. If you don't address them properly, if you don't fall in line with their belief system, or if you say the sky is blue, and they say it's purple, you'll see the heavy spirit of offensiveness make its appearance . . . and quickly! Offensiveness is like a ten-ton weight on humanity. Just like choosing to forgive others is vital to your health, so is living unoffended.

God has many things to say about how to treat our enemies—the people who persecute and hurt us. Romans 12:14 (NLT) says, "Bless those who persecute you. Don't curse them; pray that God will bless them." Yes, you read that right. . . . If someone hurts you, we need to pray that God will bless them. God also tells us to love our enemies in Luke 6:27. In Romans 12:21 (NLT), He says, "Don't let evil conquer you, but conquer evil by doing good." These are God's ways, the Creator of relationships. Man's ways bring about hurt, pain, and separation from others. God's ways bring about unity and healing. Living life unoffended means we choose to take the lower seat and elevate others above ourselves. It means focusing on pleasing God. It means remaining grateful and with a positive attitude. Just like forgiving others, it means trusting God to bring justice to the situation and the offense. Lastly, the best way to live a life free of offense is to spend time in prayer and studying God's Word. God says in Proverbs 4:20–23 (NLT):

My child, pay attention to what I say. Listen carefully to my words. Don't lose sight of them. Let them penetrate deep into your heart, for they bring life to those who find them, and healing to their whole body. Guard your heart above all else, for it determines the course of your life.

> **COMPASSION AND FORGIVENESS ARE SO POWERFUL—THEY ARE LITERAL WEAPONS IN THE SPIRIT.**

Having compassion for others can be the key to successful relationships. We've heard the saying, "We are all fighting a battle," and I believe that's true. Maybe it's a battle from the past (our soul wounds). A keen awareness that some people are just simply broken and operating from a place of hurt can help us develop deep compassion. Compassion and forgiveness are so powerful—they are literal weapons in the spirit. Having compassion goes far beyond pity. *Merriam-Webster* defines it as "sympathetic consciousness of others' distress together with a desire to alleviate it."[22] How can we alleviate someone else's distress? Love. Love = Compassion. I believe we all want it, and I believe that God gave us the ability to give it to others. We need each other. We are better together. No matter your race, gender, political stance, religious view, or economic position, nothing should separate us and stand in the way of love and compassion. We were created for relationships and to love one another.

---

22 "Compassion Definition & Meaning," *Merriam-Webster*, www.merriam-webster.com/dictionary/compassion.

PILLAR 7

PURPOSE

Here we are, returning to our metaphor of building a house and ready to complete the roof—the final pillar for attaining a balanced life . . . purpose!

Imagine building a house without a roof. How absurd would that be? It wouldn't be "complete," and it certainly would leave the rest of the house uncovered and the contents of the home left to ruin. That's how I view our purpose in life: it's the whole reason we are here, and everything we do in life requires it. You've probably asked yourself the million-dollar question: "Why am I here, and what purpose do I have?" I know I've asked myself that a time or two, and the answer seemed to change over the years (or so I thought . . . keep reading).

Have you ever stopped to think about your purpose? Do you know what it is? Take a moment, reflect, and write down your best guess. Try to keep it to just one short statement. In a little bit, I will help you discover your values and then provide an easy template for writing a purpose statement.

Don't skip ahead because I want you to write down a purpose statement now and later compare it to what you will write by the end of this chapter. Does your current day-to-day living align with what you just wrote? If not, then it's possible you need some clarity around what purpose means and what your purpose is.

There are so many books out there on discovering your purpose, or some say your "WHY." One of the best sellers in the business world is Simon Sinek's book *Start With Why*. It's geared more toward leaders, but it's a great read for anyone looking for good insight and personal development. You have to have a strong WHY to do what you do.

I remember years ago sitting in a seminar and the speaker mentioned the DO–BE–HAVE principle of living. That is, you must DO something to BE something before you will HAVE something. When I first started thinking and reading about finding your purpose, I used to think it had to do with only skill sets and certain gifts and talents that I have. I thought using (doing) my gifts and talents would certainly fulfill my purpose in life. So, I was doing something all the time.

Recently, I sat down with my father, who happens to be a world-class leadership coach, speaker, and author, and he gave me a whole new perspective on finding your purpose. He shared that when he was building his company, he was spinning on the "DO–BE–HAVE" wheel for years, thinking he had to do something to become something that would result in having something. Is that you? Are you just "doing" things to find your purpose so that you will eventually be and have all that you want? Maybe you think that if you work X number of hours, then you will be number one in your field, acquire more money, and finally have all the luxuries in life you want? So many people confuse this train of thought with fulfilling their purpose. I asked my dad what changed his perspective. He said that he felt like there was more to life than doing what the world said he should do to become something so that he would have things.

Many people that I have worked with over the years tend to think their vocation is their purpose, and it can certainly be part of it. But some folks feel stuck in a vocation that they don't enjoy and feel like they are wasting their time and not fulfilling their purpose. When this happens, a sense of stagnancy happens that often leads to some bad habits like overeating, over-drinking, lethargy, and others. What about people who have retired and feel lost with no purpose now that their careers have ended? Does it mean they are done if they aren't using their talent at work? Purpose over?

Not at all!

I worked with a woman who had recently retired from a long and successful career. She was fighting depression, which we discovered came from several things, but one source was feeling that she had lost her purpose. She had grown children and an elderly mother who needed her, but she felt she should be doing something else. Our work together led me to learn more about purpose, and I discovered it was tied to her values and who she really is—her heart. Her core. Aside from giving and doing for her family, she had a deep desire to help others in need. She wound up calling several food banks to see where she could volunteer and serve. When she did this, she felt like she was living her purpose, and like her, ALL of us have a purpose until the day we die. Her story was evidence that while skills and talents are important in finding purpose and pursuing it, it's only part of the equation. Discovering her values was really the key to living her purpose.

In Asian cultures, I have read that a person's purpose doesn't start until they are much older in years after gaining experience and wisdom that gets passed down and to the next generations to help them grow and learn. In Japanese culture, the word *ikigai* is what gets you up every morning and keeps you going. *Gai* is the key to finding your purpose or value in life. Younger people—I'm certainly not implying you have no value or purpose until you are older. Quite the contrary. You are in the process of becoming and growing. But you have to look beyond doing.

Maybe you have heard this popular Christian saying: "Man's chief end is to glorify God and to enjoy Him forever." That isn't a scripture verse, but many theologians have adapted it from scripture and used it in sermons for years. It is in THAT truth that I have found my true purpose: to glorify God. It's your purpose too. After all, He is the giver of life and has made us in His image. He gives us everything we have, including our certain gifts, skills, and talents. We are to use those gifts, talents, and skills wisely, and we are to serve and love others, not just for our own satisfaction and gain. I believe that is one of the primary ways we can bring glory to God—to love the creation God made and ultimately leave the world better while we are here.

The Bible does say in Psalm 138:8, "The LORD will fulfill His purpose for me; your steadfast love, O LORD, endures forever. Do not forsake the work of your hands." The Bible also says in Proverbs 19:21, "Many are the plans in the mind of a man, but it is the purpose of the LORD that will stand." If you are a believer in Jesus Christ and have surrendered your life to Him, He is in control. You are left with your free will, but God promises to work all things together for good (Romans 8:28). We should desire to please God, obey Him, and use all the things He has given us for good. We are a new creation; the old self is gone and the new person in Christ is in you.

In Christ, our character looks different, our values change, and our hearts become others-focused instead of self-focused. Even if you don't have a relationship with Jesus, your purpose is found in something greater than yourself to get you *outside* of yourself. We do need to use our skills, talents, and gifts to fulfill our purpose, but there is more to it. If you feel like you aren't fulfilling your purpose or lack clarity on what it is, you probably just haven't found it yet (but it's there!).

> **WE HAVE TO BECOME OUR CORE VALUES.**

As my father discovered what purpose truly is, he found that discovering your purpose starts with identifying your core values. DO-BE-HAVE was revised to BE-DO-HAVE. The more you BEcome your core values, the more you DO them. You may receive a tangible reward for hard work (which is great), but sometimes the reward lies in the satisfaction of serving and helping another human being. We have to become our core values.

The great author and leadership guru John Maxwell developed a card game that my father uses (and that I now use) to help his coaching clients identify their primary and core values and discover their purpose. Maxwell provides this list of values to help people find their purpose:

Accountable	Diversity	Independence	Simplicity
Achievement	Effectiveness	Integrity	Status
Authority	Efficiency	Knowledge	Structure
Balance	Fairness	Legacy	Teamwork
Change	Faith/Religion	Loyalty	Trust
Commitment	Family	Money/Wealth	Urgency
Competence	Fitness	Passion	Volunteerism
Courage	Fun	Perfection	Service
Creativity/Innovation	Growth	Quality	Wisdom
Customer Satisfaction	Honesty	Recognition	

Each card includes a core value. The exercise involves separating the pile into two decks. One deck represents the values that are most important to you, and the other deck represents your least important values. Next, you remove your top ten values from the first deck. Finally, you select your top five from those ten—the hills that you would die on, so to speak.

This exercise really made me think. My top five values were faith, integrity, honesty wisdom, and passion. I've run this by several people who know me best, and they all agreed those values best describe me. I had many other important values, and honestly, it was hard to narrow them down, but selecting only a few will reveal your true self and from there, you can discover your purpose. Purpose isn't so much what you're good at; it's who you are and who you are becoming. When I live out those five values, I become that person. You've heard the saying, "Actions speak louder than words." People should know who I am and what I'm about by observing me and not by what I tell them about me. You can do this using a sheet of paper without the deck of cards. I discovered that my passion is part of my purpose, and that is to add value to others. I strive to live out these values not only in my health coaching practice but with my family and friends, at church, and with whomever God brings into my life. When you add value to others, you show them you love them. By doing so, I feel that I am not only honoring them but honoring God and living out His second commandment.

> **PURPOSE ISN'T SO MUCH WHAT YOU'RE GOOD AT; IT'S WHO YOU ARE AND WHO YOU ARE BECOMING.**

And just like that, we have shifted the DO–BE–HAVE mentality to BE–DO–HAVE: When you BE something, you are better equipped to DO something; then you will HAVE something. If I am *being* a person of faith who is honest and seeks wisdom with strong passion, I continue to grow and start *doing* those things. The result is I will *have* strong relationships, a solid foundation for helping others, and a heart that has joy because I am living my purpose with integrity. For example, I am the same person at home as I am outside my home and at work. The same gifts, talents, skills, and values are implemented all the time. I feel that my main gifts and talents are listening to others, encouraging others, and giving honest feedback. I base my thoughts on God's Word, and that aligns with my core value of faith. I'm not a different person at work with clients than I am at home with my family. It may look a little different because of differing relationship dynamics but my values stay the same.

If you've never written a purpose statement, I hope you'll consider doing one. Here is a simple template that I used on my journey of discovering my purpose, and I continue to use it frequently with my clients. They love it because it's so simple. Go through the values exercise that I mentioned using a sheet of paper. When you solidify your five core values, write these two statements on a 3x5 card:

My purpose is to:

So that:

Note: The actual core value words don't have to be part of your purpose statement, but it should reflect them

Here is my purpose statement, and I feel it aligns perfectly with what I do as a health coach as well as who I am in my personal life.

My purpose is to: *Connect and add value to other people.*

So that: *They can discover their power and authority to achieve a healthy balanced life.*

My entire life is based on my FAITH. Whether at home or at work, I value HONESTY and INTEGRITY and continually seek WISDOM from God and have a driving PASSION to serve and add value to others.

The client I mentioned earlier discovered that her purpose was to volunteer and serve others in need so that they could enjoy provisions that they otherwise wouldn't have without that help.

Do you see how powerful it is to finally discover why you are here? No more wondering; just follow the simple steps and start being and doing your core values. You will naturally become the person you are meant to be. It only takes a few minutes to get alone with yourself and ask what you truly value. Using the tool above can help stimulate your thinking about different values. Think about your job or times in your life when you experienced joy about what you were doing. Maybe it's a facet of your career that you really love, like helping others learn or grow in their field. That's giving and loving. What gets you excited to get up every day and do what you do? Maybe it's not your actual job title but a task at work or home or service project that gives you great satisfaction because internally you feel in alignment with your inner self and who you are.

The opportunity to discover your purpose is much greater when you use the values template versus a skill and talent template. Purpose does not have to be limited to your vocation. You can live your purpose at home with your family, serving at your church, or volunteering like my client did. We are all created with a specific purpose on this earth. So many folks struggle with self-worth like I did for many years when I was young. If you feel worthless or are living in guilt, shame, and unforgiveness, it's hard to imagine how you can make a difference and have purpose. But I promise you, you are so valuable and have so much worth and a special purpose to give and serve others. You may have some soul wounds that need healing. This can blind us from knowing our purpose, so I always encourage that efforts be made to heal. Finding your purpose can be part of the healing process as well.

Ephesians 1:4 says, "He chose us in him before the foundation of the world, that we should be holy and blameless before him." My client was suffering from depression, and that's because the feeling of purposelessness leads to an out-of-balance life. It's very sad to think and feel like we don't have anything to contribute to life. This is why I absolutely love using the values exercise because we ALL have them. You may have made mistakes in the past but have strong remaining core values. When we live out our purpose, we are leaving a legacy, and I believe we all want to be remembered for having done something good in the world.

Many have heard of Albert Schweitzer, a theologian, philosopher, organist, and mission doctor in Africa. He received a Nobel prize in 1952, and one of his most famous quotes is this: "The purpose of human life is to serve, and to show compassion and the will to help others." This makes me think of the second greatest commandment that Jesus gave His disciples in Matthew 22:39 to "love your neighbor [others] as yourself." Remember we just talked about compassion in the last chapter on relationships. The world is built on relationships, and all of us are called to live out our purpose. Having compassion and giving back to others helps fulfill that purpose, no matter what your core values are. They are all tied to giving back and serving others.

Knowing your purpose seems elusive at times, but it doesn't have to. I hope you took some time to go through the values exercise. I hope you wrote your values down on your 3x5 card and put it where you will see it multiple times a day—and memorize them! Knowing that you were created with a specific purpose to leave the world a better place is both mind-blowing and empowering. You, yes you, possess certain values, skills, talents, and gifts that no one else has that only you can share and give to the rest of humanity. Our God is absolutely good! Everything He makes is good, and everything He does is good. In addition to spending time writing out your purpose statement, I'd like you to ask yourself a few important questions:

1) What do I want other people to remember about me and say about me when I am no longer here?
2) What will others actually remember and say?
3) Is there a discrepancy between those two answers?

If there is a discrepancy, it may be a great time for you to reevaluate and renavigate. Remember the BE–HAVE–DO model to discover who you are and your purpose. Who you are becoming? Are you positioning yourself to leave the world a better place because you lived your purpose? I pray you live your life to the highest potential and purpose that God has set in you.

AFTERWORD

Chances are, if you picked up this book, you are someone, like a lot of us, looking for simple answers to some challenging questions on what might be out of balance in your life, or why you can't seem to get your health and wellness consistently under control. My prayer is that you have taken away some things that you can start to implement today that will jumpstart the process. Keep in mind that life will never be perfect; we are only here temporarily, and if you believe and receive Jesus as your Savior, then your eternal home is in heaven. Only then will you experience perfection. While our bodies get left behind, we take our spirit and soul with us into eternity. Your gifts, talents, values, and personality will be perfected then and used for eternal purposes.

I pray that you now have a better understanding and belief that YOU have power and authority over your life, given to you by God. Now, we must use those gifts and preserve them, not give them to someone else.

I also pray that you see how discipline (not willpower) is essential for making wise choices that affect all areas of your life, like the seven pillars address.

Lastly, I pray that you walk away knowing your mandate to make our world a better place and truly bring God's kingdom here to earth. I pray that you come to know how deeply your Creator loves and values you.

Proverbs 9:1 (NIV) says, "Wisdom has built her house; she has set up its seven pillars." As you're building your "house" (your body, soul, and spirit) remember and note what spoke to you specifically in each chapter. Maybe you were strong in one or more of the pillars but possibly learned and discovered others that need some attention. You can see how neglecting things like our spirit or purpose has a profound impact on our health. I'm so grateful that God asked me to change my health coach practice to a more holistic, fully balanced approach to walking with others on their journey. God gave me those seven pillars and with good reason. He knows the areas that need strengthened in His people. He loves us all and wants our bodies healthy and well.

May you go in His *shalom*—peace, completeness, wholeness, and well-being.

www.ingramcontent.com/pod-product-compliance
Lightning Source LLC
Chambersburg PA
CBHW070545090426
42735CB00013B/3075